P9-DBY-699

THE
SECRETS
OF
JUDAS

THE
SECRETS
OF
JUDAS

The Story of the Misunderstood

Disciple and His Lost Gospel

JAMES M. ROBINSON

HarperSanFrancisco
A Division of HarperCollins*Publishers*

THE SECRETS OF JUDAS: *The Story of the Misunderstood Disciple and His Lost Gospel.* Copyright © 2006 by James M. Robinson. All rights reserved. Printed in the United States of America. No part of this book may be used or reproduced in any manner whatsoever without written permission except in the case of brief quotations embodied in critical articles and reviews. For information address HarperCollins Publishers, 10 East 53rd Street, New York, NY 10022.

HarperCollins books may be purchased for educational, business, or sales promotional use. For information please write: Special Markets Department, HarperCollins Publishers, 10 East 53rd Street, New York, NY 10022.

HarperCollins Web site: http://www.harpercollins.com
HarperCollins®, ‡®, and HarperSanFrancisco™ are
trademarks of HarperCollins Publishers.

FIRST EDITION
Designed by Joseph Rutt

Library of Congress Cataloging-in-Publication Data is available.
ISBN-13: 978–0–06–117063–8
ISBN-10: 0–06–117063–1

06 07 08 09 10 RRD (H) 10 9 8 7 6 5 4 3 2 1

Contents

The Gospel of Judas

Preface

The Gospel of Judas, a long-lost second-century fictional account that elevated Judas to hero status in the story, has been rediscovered! But it has been kept under wraps until now, to maximize its financial gain for its Swiss owners. The grand exposé is being performed by the National Geographic Society, timed for the greatest public impact, right at Easter. Those on the inside have been bought off (no doubt with considerably more than thirty pieces of silver), and sworn to silence on a stack of Bibles—or on a stack of papyrus leaves.

But it is amazing how much can be known about it by those of us on the outside looking in. This little book that you have in your hands has been written by an outsider who is not privy to the details about how *The Gospel of Judas* is being published. Many of you will read my book because you have read, or heard about, or seen on television, what the National Geographic Society is doing.

But there is a distinct advantage that I have over you, which is why, after all, you must read this book if you want to know what is really going on with *The Gospel of Judas*. For my narration is not expurgated, sanitized, cleaned up to make it an appetizing story. What has gone on in this money-making venture is not a pleasant story—about how all this has been sprung upon us, the reading and viewing public—and you have a right to know what has gone on.

I write as a scholar, and, as you will see as you read my narration, I have been involved to a very large extent over the past generation in this adventure. Yet you will also see me, in my capacity as scholar, expressing dismay, even disgust, over much of what has gone on. I lay it all out, with as much documentation as I can muster, for you to see for yourself.

I cannot promise you happy reading, but I am sure it will be exciting reading!

Integrated into the jacket design of this book and provided as a sort of frontispiece to this Preface is an image of the last page of the ancient papyrus codex dubbed *The Gospel of Judas*. The lines on the last page, below the part that is too fragmentary to reconstruct, are the heart of Judas's story and read as follows:

They made sure that they seized him during the prayer. For they were afraid of the people, because he was in all their hands as a prophet. And they approached Judas. They said to him: What are you doing in this place? Aren't you a disciple of Jesus? But he answered them according to their wishes. But Judas took some money. He delivered him over to them. >>>>>>>>>>>>>>>>>>>>>>>>>>>>>>>>
>>

THE GOSPEL
OF JUDAS

You can decipher the title at the bottom using the photograph that faces the first page of the Preface. The most obvious thing in the picture is a hole in the papyrus about the size of a penny. Just to the left of the hole, you can read, if you try hard, the Greek letters PEUA. In Coptic, they used the Greek letters, and indeed often used Greek loan words when they didn't have an appropriate Coptic synonym. So, if you can remember the shape of the Greek letters found on the fraternity and sorority houses of college campuses, you are ready: ignore the P, since that is just the Coptic definite article *The*. But what follows, EUA, is the beginning of the Greek word for "Gospel," EUAGGELION, familiar to us from our verb *evangelize*. (When U is between two vowels, it is treated as a consonant, so we transcribe it *v*; and since double-G was nasalized, i.e., pronounced *ng*, we transcribe it that way, "ng," and so: "e*v*a*ng*elize".) Then comes the hole, where once there was papyrus with the letters GG. Just to the right of the hole, you can see (if you look hard) ELION. So we transcribe the first line of the title PEUA[GG]ELION, *The Gospel*.

The second line of the title, the bottom line of the papyrus page, has the letters NI in a dark patch you cannot read, then OUDAS. The N is the Coptic genitive preposition, meaning "of." The I before the diphthong OU is a consonant, so we translate it "J." We translate the diphthong OU as a single vowel "u." And so there you have it: *Judas*. See, in just five minutes you have translated the title, *The Gospel of Judas*, and even learned a little about Coptic!

ONE

The Judas of the New Testament

Judas Iscariot is, if not the most famous, then surely the most infamous, of the inner circle of Jesus's disciples. He was one of the twelve apostles who stuck with him through thick and thin to the bitter end, until it became time to deny him three times before the cock crew twice, or tuck one's tail between one's legs and run for life back to Galilee, or, if you must, betray him. Is Judas just fulfilling biblical prophecy, implementing the plan of God for Jesus to die for our sins, doing what Jesus told him to do? Why else does he identify Jesus to the Jewish authorities with a kiss, just for thirty pieces of silver? What do the Gospels inside the New Testament—and then what does The Gospel of Judas outside the New Testament—tell us about all this?

JEWISH AND GENTILE CONFESSIONS

In order to be able to understand the presentation of Judas in the Gospels of the New Testament, it is first necessary to understand the Gospels themselves, as products of their own time, serving the purposes of churches in the last third of the first century. They were not primarily historical records, but rather were Christian witnesses to Jesus, "Gospels," "Good News." They were written for evangelizing rather than simply to inform. The Evangelists worked hard to formulate the traditions they recorded in such a way as to convey the evangelizing point they had in mind.

Since most of what we know about Judas is found in these Gospels, we must first become familiar with this evangelizing procedure of the Evangelists, before we can move back behind them half a century to talk about the historical Judas himself.

Jesus's own "public ministry" was largely confined to Jews, and his disciples were Jews. Those who had the Pentecost experience of receiving the Spirit after Easter were Jews from all over the ancient world. They had gathered in Jerusalem to celebrate a Jewish festival. And Judas was a part of this very Jewish context out of which Christianity was born.

Judaism was (and is) a very impressive ethical monotheistic religion, appealing not only to Jews, but also to Gentiles. They admired the high ethical standards of the Jewish community, and appreciated the form of worship they practiced throughout the Roman Empire: a religious service without the outdated trappings of a temple with animal sacrifice (confined to the temple in Jerusalem), but rather with an edifying, uplifting reading from their holy scriptures in Hebrew, followed by its interpretation in the everyday language of the audience. Gentiles liked to attend these services in Jewish *synagogues*, a Greek word that means "assemblies." But few of them were actually willing to convert to Judaism, to become Jews, "proselytes," by undergoing circumcision and accepting strict conformity to the Jewish lifestyle. Judaism meant abstaining from much of the desirable social life of their community! They preferred to attend the synagogue on the Sabbath, but live their normal lives the rest of the week. These Gentiles who attended the synagogue were called "God-fearers," but not "Jews."

In the Jewish synagogues where Paul preached, these God-fearers were those who were most sympathetic to his message, for he offered them precisely what they wanted from Judaism:

the high ethical ideal without animal sacrifice or outdated restrictions on their social relations. Baptism was much better than circumcision! And so the Gentile Christian Church blossomed, far surpassing in numbers what was left of Jesus's disciples in Galilee, the withering Jewish Christian Church.

Barnabas had enlisted for his mission in Antioch the most prominent convert from Judaism since Easter: the Pharisee Paul, from Tarsus on the southern coast of modern Turkey, a Jew raised out there in the Gentile world (Acts 11:25–26).

Paul and Barnabas took Titus, a Gentile convert to Christianity, with them to Jerusalem to convince the "pillars" of the Jewish Christian Church there that this Gentile, though uncircumcised, should be recognized as a fully accredited Christian (Gal. 2:3). The Jerusalem Church conceded the point (Acts 15:19–21), and reached a working arrangement with Paul and Barnabas: the original disciples would continue their mission limited to Jews, but gave the right hand of fellowship to Paul and Barnabas to continue converting uncircumcised Gentiles (Gal. 2:7–9). Paul in turn agreed to make a collection in Gentile churches for the poor of the Jerusalem Church (Gal. 2:10; Acts 11:29–30).

This fine ecumenical solution ratified by the Jerusalem Council proved difficult to implement back in the mixed congregation of Antioch, for Paul and Barnabas had in practice given up their Jewish custom of eating only among Jews to retain their ceremonial purity. Instead they ate together with all members of their mixed congregation. The Lord's Supper could not be segregated! Even Peter, there for a visit from Jerusalem, went along with this tolerant Christian practice. But Jesus's brother James, who by then had taken over the leadership of the church in Jerusalem (Acts 15:13), sent delegates to Antioch to insist that Jewish Christians should eat only at a table with Jews, to retain their ceremonial purity, even if the congregation included Gentiles (Gal. 2:12). So Peter himself withdrew to a Jews-only table, and even Barnabas went along with this segregation (Gal. 2:11–13). But Paul stood his ground, denouncing this reliance on Jewish purity as a condition for salvation (Gal. 2:14–21), and from then on did his missionary work without the support of the church of Antioch or of Jewish Christianity.

From Paul's time on, this alienation between the Jewish and Gentile branches of Christianity only got worse. The ecumenicity of the Jerusalem Council gave way to the dominance of the more numerous and prosperous Gentile Christian Church, which "returned the favor" by rejecting the small Jewish Christian Church as heretical.

By the fourth century, Epiphanius, bishop of Salamis on Cyprus, wrote against the Jewish Christians, calling them heretical sects of "Ebionites" and "Nazarenes." The first term means "the poor," the second "from Nazareth." Both were originally names for Jesus and his disciples! All these Jewish Christians were doing was continuing their Jewish lifestyle, as had Jesus, while being Christians as well. Surely, we would not call them heretics today!

JEWISH AND GENTILE GOSPELS

In the generation after Paul, each side had collected their treasured recollections of Jesus into Gospels, the Jewish Christians into their Sayings Gospel Q, and the Gentile Christians into their Narrative Gospel Mark. One main reason that the Sayings Gospel Q did not become a book within the New Testament is that the New Testament is the book of the Gentile Christian Church, not the book of the Jewish Christian Church. We know about the Sayings Gospel Q only because, as a last expression of that ecumenism, both confessions decided to merge both the Sayings Gospel Q and the Narrative Gospel Mark into a single Gospel, each from their own perspective, of course. Matthew did it from the perspective of the Jewish Christian Church, Luke from the perspective of the Gentile Christian Church. So it is possible to reconstruct rather accurately, as a team of scholars I organized for that purpose have done,[1] the Sayings Gospel Q, though no manuscripts have survived because it soon ceased to be copied by the Gentile Christian Church.

The Sayings Gospel Q made no reference at all to Judas, but the Narrative Gospel Mark, followed by the other Gospels in the New Testament, presented the familiar picture of Judas leading the Jewish authorities to the Garden of Gethsemane to arrest Jesus. But it is precisely this familiar story that needs to be reexamined, in the context of the emergence of *The Gospel of Judas*. Indeed, before *The Gospel of Judas* was rediscovered, a distinguished Mennonite scholar had already undertaken just such a reexamination: William Klassen's 1996 book *Judas: Betrayer or Friend of Jesus?* did just that.[2] All of this now calls for our own reexamination, if *The Gospel of Judas* is to be correctly understood. But first we must familiarize ourselves with the Gospels of the New Testament themselves, from which our quite understandably hostile feelings about Judas, as well as an emerging more tolerant attitude toward Judas, are both derived. We begin with the first Gentile Christian Gospel, the Gospel of Mark.

THE GENTILE GOSPEL OF MARK

Mark presents the inner circle of Jesus's disciples as being very ignorant about Jesus, as to who he was and what he was trying to do. You really have to wonder why they followed him at all—or you have to wonder why Mark portrayed them that way! So let's see how he did portray them, and try to figure out why.

After telling the Parable of the Sower, which even I can understand, Jesus asked the disciples with amazement (Mark 4:13):

Do you not understand this parable? Then how will you understand all the parables?

A whole chapter of parables follows, which Jesus has to explain rather pedantically to them (Mark 4:33–34):

> With many such parables he spoke the word to them, as they were able to hear it; he did not speak to them except in parables, but he explained everything in private to his disciples.

Yet the disciples seem still in the dark (Mark 4:40–41):

> He said to them, "Why are you afraid? Have you still no faith?" And they were filled with great awe and said to one another, "Who then is this, that even the wind and the sea obey him?"

They still don't seem to understand who Jesus was.

When the disciples in the boat see Jesus walking on the water toward the boat (Mark 6:50–52):

> . . . they all saw him and were all terrified. But immediately he spoke to them and said, "Take heart, it is I; do not be afraid." Then he got into the boat with them and the wind ceased. And they were utterly astounded, for they did not understand about the loaves, but their hearts were hardened.

Looking back on the feedings of the multitudes, Jesus asks (Mark 8:17–21):

> "Why are you talking about having no bread? Do you still not perceive or understand? Are your hearts hardened?

Do you have eyes, and fail to see? Do you have ears, and fail to hear? And do you not remember? When I broke the five loaves for the five thousand, how many baskets full of broken pieces did you collect?" They said to him, "Twelve." "And the seven for the four thousand, how many baskets full of broken pieces did you collect?" And they said to him, "Seven." Then he said to them, "Do you not yet understand?"

It is not surprising that Jesus knows just how unreliable the inner circle is (Mark 14:27–28):

And Jesus said to them, "You will all become deserters; for it is written,
　　'I will strike the shepherd, and the sheep will be scattered.'"

How many of this inner circle of the Twelve does Mark portray as being with him at the end, at the foot of the cross? None! Jesus knew quite well that none would die with him, but that they would do a quick retreat to Galilee, as Jesus told the faithful women at the tomb (Mark 16:7):

But go, tell his disciples and Peter that he is going ahead of you to Galilee; there you will see him, just as he told you.

In the Garden of Gethsemane, the inner circle had been out of it completely (Mark 14:37–41):

He came and found them sleeping; and he said to Peter, "Simon, are you asleep? Could you not keep awake one hour? Keep awake and pray that you may not come into the time of trial; the spirit indeed is willing, but the flesh is weak." And again he went away and prayed, saying the same words. And once more he came and found them sleeping, for their eyes were very heavy; and they did not know what to say to him. He came a third time and said to them, "Are you still sleeping and taking your rest? Enough! The hour has come; the Son of Man is given over into the hands of sinners. Get up, let us be going. See, the one giving me over is at hand."

With this, the antihero Judas walks across the stage. But, as our survey of Mark's presentation of the inner circle indicates, none of them are really much better in Mark's presentation than Judas! Some have thought that such a scoundrel as Judas could not possibly have been chosen by Jesus as one of the Twelve, and admitted into the innermost circle. But, from Mark's point of view, he would have fitted right in!

At least Peter should be presented favorably, since after all it is he who is the rock on which the church is built. But not in Mark—that is Matthew's effort to clean up Peter's act (Matt. 16:18)! In Mark, Peter's confession to Jesus at Caesarea Philippi, "You are the Messiah" (Mark 8:29), takes another turn (Mark 8:31–33):

Then he [Jesus] began to teach them that the Son of Man must undergo great suffering, and be rejected by the elders, the chief priest, and the scribes, and be killed, and after three days rise again. He said all this quite openly. And Peter took him aside and began to rebuke him. But turning and looking at his disciples, he rebuked Peter and said, "Get behind me, Satan! For you are setting your mind not on divine things but on human things."

Peter, not the rock, but Satan? What is going on? "Get behind me, Satan!" might fit Judas, but to refer to Peter?

On the Mount of Olives, Jesus had predicted the Twelve would abandon him (Mark 14:27–31):

> "You will all become deserters; for it is written, 'I will strike the shepherd, and the sheep will be scattered.' But after I am raised up, I will go before you to Galilee." Peter said to him, "Even though all become deserters, I will not." Jesus said to him, "Truly I tell you, this day, this very night, before the cock crows twice, you will deny me three times." But he said vehemently, "Even though I must die with you, I will not deny you." And all of them said the same.

So did Peter stick by him to the bitter end? Not according to Mark! Instead, Mark tells us (Mark 14:50):

> "They all forsook him, and fled."

When Jesus was being interrogated by the high priest, Peter followed him "at a distance" (Mark 14:54). Then Peter cops out completely (Mark 14:66–72):

> While Peter was below in the courtyard, one of the servant-girls of the high priest came by. When she saw Peter warming himself, she stared at him and said, "You also were with Jesus, the man from Nazareth." But he denied it, saying, "I do not know or understand what you are talking about." And he went out into the forecourt. Then the cock crowed. And the servant-girl, on seeing him, began again to say to the bystanders, "This man is one of them." But again he denied it. Then after a little while the bystanders again said to Peter, "Certainly you are one of them, for you are a Galilean." But he began to curse,

and he swore an oath. "I do not know this man you are talking about." At that moment the cock crowed for the second time. Then Peter remembered that Jesus had said to him, "Before the cock crows twice, you will deny me three times." And he broke down and wept.

Judging by the way Mark presents Peter, it would not have been surprising if Peter, like Judas, had gone out and killed himself, for both publicly betrayed him. Instead, Peter lived to see a better day—but not Judas!

They built the greatest cathedral in the world over the site where Peter is thought to have been buried. But Mark would not have contributed a penny to the massive fund-raising effort involved! Fortunately, that took place long after Mark's time.

Jesus's family hardly comes off much better in Mark than do the apostles. There is no infancy narrative in Mark, so the whole Christmas story is missing. Instead, the Holy Family is ashamed of Jesus, convinced that he is out of his mind, so they try to get him out of the public eye. Right after Mark's list of the twelve apostles, culminating in "Judas Iscariot, who gave him over" (Mark 3:19), Mark continued (Mark 3:19–21, 31–35):

Then he went home; and the crowd came together again, so that they could not even eat. When his family heard it, they went out to restrain him, for people were saying, "He has gone out of his mind." . . . Then his mother and his brothers came; and standing outside, they sent to him and called him. A crowd was sitting around him; and they said to him, "Your mother and your brothers and sisters are outside, asking for you." And he replied, "Who are my mother and my brothers?" And looking at those who sat around him, he said, "Here are my mother and my brothers! Whoever does the will of God is my brother and sister and mother."

The "Holy Family"? Hardly in Mark! Does Mark present Judas as all that much worse than the Holy Family? The same put-down applied to Jesus's hometown, Nazareth (Mark 6:1–6).

Judas Iscariot fits all too well into Mark's portrayal not only of the twelve apostles, especially Peter, but also of the Holy Family and his hometown! What is going on here?

Mark was the first Evangelist of the thriving Gentile Christian Church, as it became increasingly alienated from the Jewish Christian Church built with Jesus's original disciples. Put into that context, it is less surprising that Mark so decidedly puts down the Twelve and the Holy Family. One can only recall the strained relations reflected already by Paul (Gal. 1:15–19; 2:1–14).

Should one expect the Gospel of the Gentile Church to be more favorable than was Paul toward Peter ("Cephas"), whom Paul "opposed to his face, because he stood self-condemned," and toward the "circumcision faction," "this hypocrisy," those who were "not acting consistently with the truth of the gospel," not to speak of the "false believers" who opposed Paul in Jerusalem? After all, Paul had warned explicitly against any other gospel than his own (Gal. 1:6–9).

One would actually expect a Gentile Christian Gospel to be anything but enthusiastic about those whom Paul put down so decidedly! The portrayal in Paul's Letter to the Galatians of the Twelve ("Cephas and John"), specifically Peter ("Cephas") and the Holy Family ("James"), fits perfectly the negative portrayal of the Twelve, Peter, and the Holy Family in the Gentile Gospel Mark. One should not expect it to be otherwise. But then the question has to be raised as to whether these Markan portrayals do full justice to these persons, or whether they are the victims of Paul's, and Mark's, theology. And what does this then suggest about Mark's portrayal of another one of the Twelve, Judas Iscariot?

• • •

The Gospel of Mark has been characterized as "a passion narrative with a long introduction." What this characterization has in mind is the way in which Mark seems to have his focus on the cross long before the actual crucifixion story itself. Already very early on, the plot to kill Jesus is brought into the story (Mark 3: 6):

> The Pharisees went out and immediately conspired with the Herodians against him, how to destroy him.

Then, the second half of Mark is dominated by Jesus again and again predicting his crucifixion in all too much detail even for Peter, namely (Mark 8:31–32):

> Then he began to teach them that the Son of Man must undergo great suffering, and be rejected by the elders, the chief priests, and the scribes, and be killed, and after three days rise again. He said all this quite openly.

Then on the descent from the Mount of Transfiguration, Jesus casually mentions his resurrection to Peter, James, and John, who had been with him there (Mark 9:9):

> As they were coming down the mountain, he ordered them to tell no one about what they had seen, until after the Son of Man had risen from the dead. So they kept the matter to themselves, questioning what this rising from the dead could mean.

Had he not just told them that after three days he would rise again?

Shortly thereafter, there is a second detailed prediction of Good Friday and Easter (Mark 9:30–32):

He was teaching his disciples, saying to them, The Son of Man is to be given over into human hands, and they will kill him, and three days after being killed, he will rise again. But they did not understand what he was saying and were afraid to ask him.

Then, a third time, Jesus describes in even more detail what is going to happen (Mark 10:32–34):

He took the twelve aside again and began to tell them what was to happen to him, saying, "See, we are going up to Jerusalem, and the Son of Man will be handed over to the chief priests and the scribes, and they will condemn him to death; then they will hand him over to the Gentiles; they will mock him, and spit upon him, and flog him, and kill him; and after three days he will rise again."

For all practical purposes, this is a rather detailed summary of Mark's passion and resurrection narratives (Mark 15–16). Indeed, it is generally recognized that such a detailed prediction was not made by the historical Jesus himself, but rather was formulated by the Evangelist and put on Jesus's tongue.

Even the Pauline gospel, limited to preaching only "Christ crucified" (1 Cor. 1:23; 2:2), crops up once in Mark on Jesus's tongue (Mark 10:45):

For the Son of Man came not to be served but to serve, and to give his life a ransom for many.

After all these allusions to the crucifixion, not to speak of detailed narrations, the Markan Jesus could quite understandably mention at the Last Supper (Mark 14:21): "The Son of Man goes as it is written of him." And Judas would only have to be a bit smarter than Peter and the other apostles to know that it was the will of God that Jesus die for our sins in accordance with the scriptures (1 Cor. 15:3).

In view of Mark's portrayal of Jesus's death as the fulfillment of prophecy and as being the will of God of which Jesus and the Twelve were fully aware, with Jesus acquiescing to God's will even to the point of death, it is really surprising, not that Judas turned Jesus over to the authorities to kill him as part of the plan of God, but that Mark can even present this in a reproachful way (Mark 14:18–21):

> And when they had taken their places and were eating, Jesus said, "Truly I tell you, one of you will give me over, one who is eating with me." They began to be distressed and to say to him one after another, "Surely, not I?" He said to them, "It is one of the twelve, one who is dipping bread into the bowl with me. For the Son of Man goes as it is written of him, but woe to the one by whom the Son of Man is given over! It would have been better for that one not to have been born."

But then, according to Mark, if Judas Iscariot had never been born, how would the scripture have been fulfilled, how would the will of God have been done, how would Jesus have "died for our sins in accordance with the scriptures" (1 Cor. 15:3)? Why pronounce a woe on Judas, who is only doing what he was born to do?—what God, and therefore Jesus, want him to do?

Mark explains that the Jewish authorities want to kill Jesus, but need to find a way to arrest him privately (Mark 14:1–2):

> The chief priests and the scribes were looking for a way to arrest Jesus by stealth and kill him; for they said, "Not during the festival, or there may be a riot among the people."

Jesus picks this up to mock them at the arrest—and to emphasize that all they are doing is fulfilling the scriptures (Mark 14:48–50):

> "Have you come out as against a robber, with swords and clubs to capture me? Day after day I was with you in the temple teaching, and you did not seize me. But let the scripture be fulfilled." And they all forsook him, and fled.

Thus Judas is aiding the Jewish authorities' arrest of Jesus in order to kill him. This cannot be, from Mark's point of view, just an innocent referral to the religious authorities to hear what Jesus has to say, such as is appropriate on any and every issue that arises within Judaism. Their intention is not to interview Jesus to learn who he is and what he is trying to do, whereupon they might agree with him and release him. They only want to "arrest Jesus by stealth and kill him" (Mark 14:2). This had been their intention from the very beginning, when the Pharisees and Herodians conspired together "how to destroy him" (Mark 3:6). So, from Mark's point of view, Judas is at best a party to the crime. Mark can't completely whitewash the scene by presenting Judas Iscariot as just doing the will of God and so the will of Jesus.

The Gospel of Mark presents in graphic detail the scene in the Garden of Gethsemane, where Judas plays the central role (Mark 14:43–45):

> And immediately, while he was still speaking, Judas came, one of the twelve, and with him a crowd with swords and clubs, from the chief priests and the scribes and the elders. Now the one who gave him over had given them a sign, saying, The one I shall kiss is the man; seize him and lead him away under guard. And when he came, he went up to him at once, and said, Master! And he kissed him. And they laid hands on him and seized him.

It is of course this text that is primarily responsible for the "bad press" Judas Iscariot has received ever since.

THE JEWISH SAYINGS GOSPEL Q

The Jewish Christian Church of the first generation spoke primarily Aramaic, of which no written texts have survived. After all, most of the original disciples were illiterate! But, fortunately, somewhere along the way they did translate Jesus's sayings into Greek, no doubt for use in their mission among Greek-speaking Jews. They even brought them together into a small collection of Jesus's sayings. So I have spent the last two decades reconstructing it, with a group of scholars I brought together for this purpose. Let me explain:

The Critical Edition of Q, which we published in 2000, presents this written text of sayings ascribed to Jesus. It is not a book that exists today in its own right in the New Testament. Instead, it lurks just below the surface, and has to be reconstructed. This is how: both Matthew and Luke had copies of the Sayings Gospel Q, and used it, together with the Gospel of Mark, in composing their Gospels, as a kind of "ecumenical" gesture, Matthew from the point of view of the Jewish Christians, Luke from the point of view of the Gentile Christians. So when Matthew and Luke have the same saying of Jesus, but they cannot have gotten it from Mark (since it is not in Mark), they must have gotten it from another source. Scholars a century ago nicknamed this other source "Q," the first letter of the German word meaning "source," *Quelle*. Today we refer to it as the Sayings Gospel Q, to distinguish it from the four Narrative Gospels with which we are familiar from the New Testament: Matthew, Mark, Luke, and John.

Since Q itself does not have chapter and verse numbers, we make use of Luke's chapter and verse numbers when quoting

Q. This is because Luke follows Q's sequence more faithfully than does Matthew. Since there is no birth narrative in Q, the text of Q begins at Luke 3 with John the Baptist. So the first chapter of Q is called Q 3. Q material is scattered through Matthew and Luke, but ends just before the passion narrative in Luke 22. So the last chapter of Q is Q 22.

Since the Sayings Gospel Q is composed for use in the actual continuation of Jesus's own message by his disciples, it does not look back on Jesus's public ministry so much as a past reality to be described, as it is a collection of sayings still to be proclaimed. What is important is not who said what to whom, but that these sayings are decisive for you—your fate hangs on hearkening to them! It is perhaps for this reason that it does not mention by name those who carry on the message. None of the Twelve is mentioned by name, not even Peter—and not Judas!

THE JEWISH CHURCH'S ECUMENICAL GOSPEL OF MATTHEW

The Gospel of Matthew seems to have been written when the remaining vestiges of the Jewish Church of Q merged into the much larger Gentile Church of Mark. The merging of the Gospels of the two communions was a kind of ecumenical gesture attesting to the hoped-for harmonizing of the two confessions.

Matthew supplements the Markan record about Judas in significant ways. Mark had ascribed the initiative for the bribe to the chief priests (Mark 14:11). But in Matthew, Judas actually asks the chief priests to offer him a bribe (Matt 26:15): "What will you give me if I give him over to you?" And Matthew focuses on Judas at the Last Supper when it comes to identifying who will give him over (Matt. 26:25):

Judas, who gave him over, said, "Surely not I, Rabbi?" He replied, "You have said so."

This is not fully explicit, but nonetheless the reader gets the message: Judas will do it.

It is quite significant that Matthew presents Judas here as addressing Jesus as *Rabbi*, rather than the Greek translation "Lord" normally used in the Gospels. Of course it may very well be that in the Aramaic used at the Last Supper, and elsewhere, Jesus was in fact addressed as *Rabbi*. At that time it did not yet have the specialized modern meaning of Jewish clergy, but was just a Jewish term of respect for a religious leader.

But there seems to be a clear aversion to *Rabbi* or *Rabbouni* on the part of Matthew and Luke: once when Mark uses *Rabbouni* of Jesus (Mark 10:51), both Matthew and Luke read "Lord" (Matt. 9:28; Luke 18:41). Another time when Mark presents Peter addressing Jesus in the transfiguration story as *Rabbi* (Mark 9:5), Matthew and Luke read "Lord" (Matt. 17:4; Luke 9:33). In still another Markan instance of Peter addressing Jesus as *Rabbi* (Mark 11:21), Matthew omits the address (Matt. 21:20), and Luke omits the whole incident.

It is only when Mark presents Judas addressing Jesus as *Rabbi* (Mark 14:45) that Matthew retains *Rabbi* (Matt. 26:49); Luke omits here the address completely (Luke 22:47). In fact, Luke never uses *Rabbi* anywhere. His is the Gospel most emphatically addressed to Gentiles! But Matthew actually inserts a second instance of Judas addressing Jesus as *Rabbi* (Matt. 26:25), where there is no parallel at all in the other Gospels. This is obviously because Matthew has disowned Judas. Such a form of address on the part of Judas merely documents his status as an unworthy disciple.

Actually, Matthew explicitly rejects the use of *Rabbi*, by arguing that teachers of the Law and Pharisees seek to be so addressed out of pride (Matt. 23:5–7):

They do all their deeds to be seen by others; for they make their phylacteries broad and their fringes long. They love to have the place of honor at banquets and the best seats in the synagogues, and to be greeted with respect in the marketplaces, and to have people call them *Rabbi*.

It is hence to be avoided (Matt. 23:8):

But you are not to be called *Rabbi*, for you have one teacher, and you are brethren.

So Matthew emphasizes that it is Judas who calls Jesus *Rabbi*!

When Judas actually kisses Jesus in the Garden of Gethsemane to identify him to the Jewish authorities, Matthew has Jesus add (Matt. 26:50): "Friend, do what you are here to do." This is almost an exoneration of Judas for the identifying kiss! The irony of the scene is that Jesus addresses him as "friend," an extremely rare term on Jesus's lips!

Then Matthew, alone among the Gospels, reports the remorse of Judas. He returns the money to the chief priests and elders, saying (Matt. 27:4): "I have sinned in giving over innocent blood." Then, when they shrug their shoulders, Judas, "throwing down the pieces of silver in the temple, departed; and he went and hanged himself" (Matt. 27:5).

Matthew, as a Jewish Gospel, would of course have every reason to present a more favorable view of the Jewish disciples of Jesus than do Paul and Mark. After all, it was Matthew who rescued Peter from being Satan, to let him be the rock (Matt. 16:18–19):

And I tell you, you are Peter, and on this rock I will build my church, and the gates of Hades will not prevail against it. I will give you the keys of the kingdom of heaven, and whatever you bind on earth will be bound in heaven, and whatever you loose on earth will be loosed in heaven.

To be sure, Matthew retains Peter's opposition to the idea of the passion, and lets Peter still receive the rebuke "Satan." But Matthew did flesh out the dialogue to make it less shocking and more understandable (Matt. 16:22–23):

> And Peter took him aside and began to rebuke him, saying, "God forbid it, Lord! This must never happen to you." But he turned and said to Peter, "Get behind me, Satan! You are a hindrance to me; for you are setting your mind not on divine things but on human things."

Here the Markan criticism is retained, but put in a context that mitigates it somewhat. To justify Peter's rejection of the idea of the passion, his very understandable comment is added: "God forbid it, Lord! This must never happen to you." And Jesus's explanation justifying his rebuke is added: "You are a hindrance to me."

Matthew of course had every reason to clear Peter's name, since, after all, Peter is, of course after Jesus, the hero of his Gospel. If Mark might have been the first to cast a stone at Peter, Matthew would have been the first to lay a cornerstone at the cathedral of St. Peter in Rome.

THE GENTILE CHURCH'S ECUMENICAL GOSPEL OF LUKE

Luke presented the public ministry of Jesus as a sort of idealized time, a period not only quite different from the time before Jesus's public ministry, but also quite different from Luke's own time long after Jesus's public ministry.

We are quite familiar with Luke's way of idealizing the beginnings of the church after Easter as a wonderful time, but a time that did not continue down into his present. In Luke's book of Acts, the beginning of the church is idealized, with a kind of voluntary sharing of all goods and funds, almost a Christian kind of communism. However, this is no longer the practice in Luke's own time. It was just the beginning of the church, which he looked back on with admiration and nostalgia, but not as a way of life to follow now. It was not a time to imitate.

Luke presented Jesus's public ministry in a similar way, as an idealized time in the past that does not really apply to the present. Luke reports that after failing in the temptation, the devil left Jesus "until an opportune time" (Luke 4:13). The devil found that opportune time just before the passion narrative, when Satan reappeared just in time to enter Judas (Luke 22:3) and to tempt Peter (Luke 22:31). The period of the devil's absence, corresponding to the public ministry of Jesus, is for Luke a paradise-like unrepeatable idyllic period of time, much like the idealized beginning of the Christian Church.

This idealized time, free of the devil, corresponds very closely to the limits of Q in Luke. Q began at Luke 3:2, with John the Baptist, and went through Luke 22:30, just before the passion narrative. Indeed, the idyllic period of time ends in the very next verse after Q ends. Immediately after quoting the conclusion of Q in Luke 22:30, Luke presents Satan reemerging to tempt Peter and give Jesus over in Luke 22:31. Then Luke revokes quite explicitly the mission instructions of Q (quoted in Luke 10:1–16). Those mission instructions had stated (Q 10:4):

Carry no purse, nor knapsack, nor sandals, nor stick, and greet no one on the road.

Just listen to Luke revoking these mission instructions, to get ready for the passion narrative (Luke 22:35–38):

> And he said to them, "When I sent you out with no purse or bag or sandals, did you lack anything?" They said, "Nothing." He said to them, "But now, let him who has a purse take it, and likewise a bag. And let him who has no sword sell his mantle and buy one. For I tell you that this scripture must be fulfilled in me, 'And he was reckoned with transgressors'; for what is written about me has its fulfillment." And they said, "Look, Lord, here are two swords." And he said to them, "It is enough."

In this way Luke prepares for Mark's immediately following report of the arrest (Mark 14:46–47):

> But one of those who stood near drew his sword and struck the slave of the high priest, cutting off his ear.

So, by rearming the disciples, Luke has closed down the epoch of Q, wonderful though it may have seemed, and re-entered the "real world" of push and shove. With Q safely behind him, Luke can proceed to follow Mark through the passion narrative, and move on into the Gentile Church's mission practices, which Luke exemplified in the book of Acts, in his portrayal of Paul moving about throughout the whole Hellenistic world.

This periodizing of history into an idealized past and a realistic present did not require Luke to omit the mission instructions of Q, though they were now outdated and formally abrogated by Jesus himself. Rather, Luke preserved them in their most archaic form (Luke 10:1–16). He had not been called upon to update them to conform to current practice, as had Matthew. Matthew, clinging longer to the older procedures, had to make the adjustments called for by the passage of time. Most prominently, Matthew justified, by appealing to Jesus's instructions, a mission limited to Jews, a Jewish mission carried out to the exclusion of Gentiles and Samaritans, probably almost up until Matthew's own time (Matt. 10:5b–6, 23):

> Go nowhere among the Gentiles, and enter no town of the Samaritans, but go rather to the lost sheep of the house of Israel. . . . When they persecute you in one town, flee to the next; for truly I tell you, you will not have gone through all the towns of Israel before the Son of Man comes.

It is this Jews-only mission that one must presuppose was still being carried out by the Jerusalem Church, at the time James sent delegates to Antioch to enforce the segregated policy at the Lord's Supper in Antioch, which Paul had so strenuously opposed.

In the Gospel of Luke, Jesus does not say to Peter, "Get behind me, Satan!" This scene would come right after Luke 9:22, to be parallel to Mark 8:33, but is completely missing. Satan tried to get hold of Peter, but Jesus protected him (Luke 22:31–32):

> Simon, Simon, listen! Satan has demanded to sift all of you like wheat, but I have prayed for you that your own faith may not fail, and you, when you have turned back, strengthen your brothers.

But Satan has instead gotten a grip on Judas (Luke 22:3):

> Then Satan entered into Judas called Iscariot, who was one of the twelve; he went away and conferred with the chief priests and officers of the temple police about how he might give him over to them. They were greatly pleased

and agreed to give him money. So he consented and began
to look for an opportunity to give him over to them when
no crowd was present.

One would think that Judas, into whom Satan had entered,
would have been the most obvious candidate for an exorcism,
such as Jesus performed most dramatically for an epileptic boy
(Mark 9:17–29).

Even the disciples become adept at exorcism. On their return
from the mission of the seventy, they report (Luke 10:17–18):

> The seventy returned with joy, saying, "Lord, in your
> name even the demons submit to us!" He said to them, "I
> watched Satan fall from heaven like a flash of lightning."

The best-known disciple from whom Jesus had cast out a
demon, or, more precisely, seven demons, is of course Mary
Magdalene (Luke 8:1–3):

> The twelve were with him, as well as some women
> who had been cured of evil spirits and infirmities: Mary,
> called Magdalene, from whom seven demons had gone
> out, and Joanna, the wife of Herod's steward Chuza, and
> Suzanna, and many others, who provided for them out
> of their resources.

It is difficult to imagine Judas really being possessed by a
demon, or even by Satan, and Jesus or one of the apostles not
freeing him of that possession. Put otherwise, Luke's talk of
Satan entering Judas sounds more like Luke's put-down than a
historical fact. Judas wasn't really a demoniac.

Luke modifies significantly, though in small details, the
Markan report of Jesus speaking of the one who would betray
him (Matt. 22:21–22):[3]

But see, the one who betrays me is with me, and his hand is on the table. For the Son of Man is going as it has been determined, but woe to that one by whom he is betrayed.

Just whose hand is on the table is not made clear, but it replaces Mark's reference to someone who dips into the dish with Jesus, which is where John clearly identifies Judas (John 13:26). Luke then adds that after Jesus said that one at the table with him would give him over (Luke 22:23):

They began to question one another, which of them it was that would do this.

But rather than following this up by pointing to Judas, as does Matthew (Matt. 26:25), Luke instead inserts here a scene found earlier in Mark (Mark 10:41–45): the disciples argue about which of them was to be regarded as greatest (Luke 22:24–30), triggered in Mark by the request of James and John for places on each side of Jesus in his glory (Mark 10:38–40). This was so awkward that Matthew had transferred it to a request by their mother (Matt. 20:20–23), and Luke omits it completely, only to insert the ensuing discussion of true greatness into the Last Supper, rather than going on to identify Judas as the one who would give him over.

In the Garden of Gethsemane, Luke adds the fact that Judas was *leading* the crowd (Luke 22:47). As Judas comes to kiss Jesus, Jesus recognizes this act as the sign to the Jewish authorities (Luke 22:48):

Judas, is it with a kiss that you are giving over the Son of Man?

Judas promptly disappears from the scene, but instead one finds the Markan story of a disciple cutting off the right ear of

a slave of the high priest, whereupon Luke has Jesus reproach
the unnamed disciple (Luke 22:51):

> But Jesus said, "No more of this!" And he touched his ear
> and healed him.

Such an act of kindness to a person who had come to arrest him
is worthy of Pope John Paul II forgiving the person who tried to
assassinate him. Indeed, at the crucifixion only Luke presents
Jesus saying (Luke 23:34):

> Father, forgive them; for they do not know what they are
> doing.

Just where this leaves Judas is not made clear. For Luke, Judas
paid the price for what he did (Acts 1:18):

> Now this man acquired a field with the reward of his
> wickedness; and falling headlong, he burst open in the
> middle and all his bowels gushed out.

THE GOSPEL OF JOHN

It is decidedly the Gospel of John that bears most of the responsibility for discrediting Judas completely. Here is the way he
does it (John 6:64–71):

> "But among you there are some who do not believe."
> For Jesus knew from the first who were the ones that did
> not believe, and who was the one that would give him
> over. And he said, "For this reason I have told you that no
> one can come to me unless it is granted by the Father."
> Because of this many of his disciples turned back and no
> longer went about with him. So Jesus asked the twelve,

"Do you also wish to go away?" Simon Peter answered him, "Lord, to whom can we go? You have the words of eternal life. We have come to believe and know that you are the Holy One of God." Jesus answered them, "Did I not choose you, the twelve? Yet one of you is a devil." He was speaking of Judas son of Simon Iscariot, for he, though one of the twelve, was going to give him over.

The frequent question as to why Jesus would have included Judas in his inner circle is thus most acute in the Gospel of John. If Jesus knew "from the first" that Judas would give him over, he must have included him for that very purpose!

Just as Luke had transferred Peter being called Satan (Mark 8:33) into Judas being possessed by Satan (Luke 22:3), just so John presents Judas being possessed by Satan. He smuggles this "detail" into the story much earlier than at the Last Supper:

There is a familiar scene of Jesus at the home of Simon the leper in Bethany (Mark 14:3–9), or, as Luke has it, at the home of Simon the Pharisee much earlier, in Galilee (Luke 7:36). A woman (Luke 7:37: a prostitute), carrying an alabaster jar of very costly ointment of nard, pours it over his head (Luke 7:38: his feet), whereupon those present (Luke 7:39: the Pharisee) are indignant at the waste. If one can thus see how Luke changes a story in the home of a leper into something that fits better his polemic against the Pharisees, it should come as no surprise to find that the Gospel of John transforms much the same story to serve his purposes as a polemic against Judas.

John takes the familiar story of Jesus in the home of Mary and Martha (Luke 10:38–42), where Mary is praised for her attentive listening to Jesus, rather than just serving him at table, and turns it into a polemic against—Judas (John 12:1–8):

Six days before the Passover Jesus came to Bethany, the home of Lazarus, whom he had raised from the dead. There they gave a dinner for him. Martha served, and Lazarus was one of those at the table with him. Mary took a pound of costly perfume made of pure nard, anointed Jesus's feet, and wiped them with her hair. The house was filled with the fragrance of the perfume. But Judas Iscariot, one of his disciples (the one who was about to give him over), said, "Why was this perfume not sold for three hundred denarii and the money given to the poor?" (He said this not because he cared about the poor, but because he was a thief; he kept the common purse and used to steal what was put in it.) Jesus said, "Leave her alone. She bought it so that she might keep it for the day of my burial. You always have the poor with you, but you do not always have me."

Here it is quite obvious that Luke, and then John, take a story from the tradition about Jesus and, by changing the characters and plot, makes it serve their polemical purposes. This should then make it equally clear that the damning of Judas, as the keeper of the moneybags, who only pretends to care for the poor so as to steal money from Jesus and the other disciples, is more probable as a creation of John than as a historical fact. At the Last Supper John needs only to mention that the devil had already inspired Judas to give him over (John 13:2), and more pointedly John writes that Satan entered Judas when Jesus gave him bread he had dipped into the dish (John 13:27).

The Gospel of John has Jesus identify Judas as the one to give him over, already at the beginning of the parting discourse held at the Last Supper (John 13:1–2, 4–11, 18–19, 21–30):

Jesus knew that his hour had come to depart from this world and go to the Father. Having loved his own who were in the world, he loved them to the end. The devil had already put it into the heart of Judas son of Simon

Iscariot to give him over. And during supper Jesus . . .
got up from the table, took off his outer robe, and tied a
towel around himself. Then he poured water into a basin
and began to wash the disciples' feet and to wipe them
with the towel that was tied around him. . . . Jesus said to
him [Simon Peter], "One who has bathed does not need to
wash, except for the feet, but is entirely clean. And you
are clean, though not all of you." For he knew who was to
betray him. . . . "I am not speaking of all of you; I know
whom I have chosen. But it is to fulfill the scripture, 'The
one who ate my bread has lifted his heel against me.' I
tell you this now, before it occurs, so that when it does
occur, you may believe that I am he." . . . After saying this
Jesus was troubled in spirit, and declared, "Very truly, I
tell you, one of you will betray me." The disciples looked
at one another, uncertain of whom he was speaking. One
of his disciples—the one whom Jesus loved—was reclin-
ing next to him; Simon Peter therefore motioned to him
to ask Jesus of whom he was speaking. So while reclin-
ing next to Jesus, he asked him, "Lord, who is it?" Jesus
answered, "It is the one to whom I give this piece of bread
when I have dipped it in the dish." So when he had dipped
the piece of bread, he gave it to Judas son of Simon Iscariot.
After he received the piece of bread, Satan entered into
him. Jesus said to him, "Do quickly what you are going
to do." Now no one at the table knew why he said this
to him. Some thought that, because Judas had the common purse, Jesus was telling him, "Buy what we need
for the festival"; or, that he should give something to the
poor. So, after receiving the piece of bread, he immediately went out. And it was night.

In the so-called high priestly prayer with which Jesus's parting
discourse concludes, there is a flashback to Judas (John 17:12):

While I was with them, I protect them in your name that
you have given me. I guarded them, and not one of them
was lost except the son of destruction, so that the scripture might be fulfilled.

The final scene of Judas in the Gospel of John is at the arrest
(John 18:1–12):

After Jesus had spoken these words, he went out with his
disciples across the Kidron valley to a place where there
was a garden, which he and his disciples entered. Now
Judas, who gave him over, also knew the place, because
Jesus often met there with his disciples. So Judas brought a
detachment of soldiers together with police from the chief
priests and the Pharisees, and they came there with lan-
terns and torches and weapons. Then Jesus, knowing all
that was to happen to him, came forward and asked them,
"Whom are you looking for?" They answered, "Jesus of
Nazareth." Jesus replied, "I am he." Judas, who gave him
over, was standing with them. When Jesus said to them,
"I am he," they stepped back and fell to the ground. Again
he asked them, "Whom are you looking for?" And they
said, "Jesus of Nazareth." Jesus answered, "I told you that
I am he. So if you are looking for me, let these men go."
This was to fulfill the word that he had spoken, "I did
not lose a single one of those whom you gave me." Then
Simon Peter, who had a sword, drew it, struck the high
priest's slave, and cut off his right ear. The slave's name
was Malchus. Jesus said to Peter, "Put your sword back
into its sheath. Am I not to drink the cup that the Father
has given me?" So the soldiers, their officer, and the Jewish police arrested Jesus and bound him.

Here Judas plays his indispensable role in the story, of bringing the Jewish authorities to arrest Jesus. But his role is, compared to in the other Gospels, minimal. There is no kiss of death. He does his thing and disappears from history, as far as the Gospel of John is concerned.

JUDAS IN THE CANONICAL GOSPELS AND ACTS

From this survey of the canonical Gospels and the book of Acts, one can see how each handles the figure of Judas, both in the sense that they are the genesis of the horrible image of Judas down through the centuries, and the sense that upon inspection they do not present that image as being as horrible as we have usually assumed.

To be sure, they do not in any sense of the word vindicate him, much less make him into the hero, as apparently *The Gospel of Judas* would try to do. Modern efforts point out that he is not (with the one exception of Luke 6:16) actually said to betray Jesus as a "traitor," and that he is only carrying out his role as prophesied in the Hebrew scriptures, predicted by Jesus, even ordered by Jesus. But the canonical texts also pronounce a woe on him for his evil deed, and present him in such remorse that he kills himself. This is not what one normally does in fulfilling the Hebrew scriptures or obeying Jesus! But a presentation in which Judas is to be praised, not blamed, calls for a rather complete reversal of values, such as we await in *The Gospel of Judas.*

TWO

The Historical Judas

THE NAME JUDAS ISCARIOT

Judas is the Greek spelling of the Hebrew name *Judah*, meaning "praised." Judah is about as popular a name as one can find in all of Judaism. Indeed, Judaism itself is named after Judah! Judah is, after all, the origin of the word *Jew*. Paul points out that he grew up "in Judaism" (Gal. 1:13–14), though he was of the tribe of Benjamin (Phil. 3:5).

Judah was the fourth son of Jacob and Leah, and Judah was the name of one of the twelve tribes of Israel. When the Israelites entered the Promised Land, the tribe of Judah was awarded the southern part. After the reign of Solomon, the Israelite kingdom that David had created was divided into two kingdoms: Judah was the southern kingdom and Israel the northern kingdom. The northern kingdom was overrun by the Assyrians and disappeared from the pages of history. But after the Babylonian captivity of the southern kingdom, Judah was repopulated by those who returned from captivity. The Roman emperor Augustus named it Judaea, and so its inhabitants became "Judeans" (John 7:1). In our day, Judea is the name used by the modern state of Israel to designate its southern part, though the United Nations, the United States, and hence the media, usually refer to much of it as part of the "occupied West Bank."

Understandably enough, Judas, as the Greek spelling of the Hebrew word *Judah*, was a very popular Jewish name indeed. The Maccabean revolt against Syrian armies was led by Judas Maccabee (167–160 BCE), and of course the name was especially popular among the Maccabeans. The Jewish historian Josephus reports that the terrorists of his day, the Zealots, whom Josephus calls Sicarii, often used the name Judas for their leaders. In the New Testament, six people named Judas are mentioned.

Actually, Jesus had a brother named Judas. This has been somewhat hidden from view by the fact that the translators of the King James Bible wanted, at all costs, to keep the two persons named Judas separate. So the King James Bible entitled the Epistle ascribed to Jesus's brother as "Jude." The Epistle begins: "Jude, a servant of Jesus Christ and brother of James." James is of course another brother of Jesus, as the list in Matthew 13:55 indicates:

> Is not this the carpenter's son? Is not his mother called Mary? And are not his brothers James and Joseph and Simon and Judas?

Furthermore, in Luke's list of the twelve apostles, two are named Judas (Luke 6:16):

> . . . and Judas the son of James, and Judas Iscariot, who became a traitor.

Of course, after the crucifixion when Luke lists only eleven apostles, there is only one Judas (Acts 1:13):

> . . . and Judas the son of James.

Because of the number of persons named Judas, and especially because there are two named Judas in Luke's list of the Twelve, not to speak of Jesus's brother Judas, it was obviously necessary to distinguish one Judas from the other. One may compare the various lists of the Twelve: most apostles are given only one name. But when there are more than one with the same name, for example Simon Peter and Simon the Cananaean, or James the brother of Andrew and James the son of Alphaeus, these clarifications are appended to their names to distinguish between them. So it is with Judas the son of James and Judas Iscariot.

What then does *Iscariot* mean? There are various theories, so many in fact that none can be counted on as definitive.

Perhaps it means "man (Ish-) from Karioth," if that really is the name of a town of southern Judea mentioned in Joshua 15:25. But what is written there could just mean "town," as suggested by the rather free New Revised Standard Version translation, "Kerioth-hezron (that is, Hazor)." The New Revised Standard Version also lists, in a note to "Judas son of Simon Iscariot" (John 6:71), a second choice: "Judas son of Simon from Karyot (Kerioth)." There is a Tel Qirrioth on the current map in the Negev. And there is an Askaroth or Askar near Shechem. Another suggestion has been that it just meant a person from the "city," i.e. Jerusalem, as attested in later Jewish sources. Any of these derivations would make Judas the only one of the twelve apostles from Judea, and would help explain how it was that he was known to the Jerusalem authorities.

Or *Iscariot* may mean one of the Sicarii, the name Josephus used for the Zealots of his day. And there are still other explanations for *Iscariot*. In sum, there is so much uncertainty about the derivation of the term that nothing can be made of it, other than that it was used to distinguish this Judas both from the other Judas listed among the Twelve and from Jesus's brother Judas.

The Gospel of John also lists the name of Judas's father. For it was customary then, just as it is now, to use a father's name (or ancestor's name) as the "second" name of a person. My own name has two such "patronymics." Of course "–son" is the most common English way to produce a patronymic. Robinson goes back to the Scottish nickname for Robert, Robin. But even my middle name, McConkey, uses the Gaelic patronymic, Mc or Mac. In Greek, the patronymic is put in the genitive, meaning "X (the son) of Y." So the Gospel of John refers to "Judas (son of) Simon Iscariot" (John 6:71; 13:2, 26). But since this Simon is unknown, that bit of information does not help us further.

JUDAS IN THE INNER CIRCLE

There is of course discussion as to whether Judas was one of "the Twelve." It has seemed to many that it would be unreasonable for Jesus to admit such a person into that inner circle. Yet the Gospel of John, which is the Gospel that is most critical of Judas, explicitly scores the point that Jesus did choose him (John 6:70):

> Jesus answered them, "Did I not choose you, the twelve? Yet one of you is a devil." He was speaking of Judas son of Simon Iscariot.

But John's having to score the point that Jesus really did choose him assumes Judas to have been a notorious scoundrel, which is precisely what one would like to question.

Celsus, a Jewish critic of Christianity in the second century, used Jesus's betrayal by a disciple as a reason to discredit Jesus:[1]

> How could we have accepted as God one who, as was reported, did not carry out any of the works he announced, and when we had evidence against him and denounced him and wanted to punish him he hid himself and tried

to escape; who was captured in a disgraceful manner and even was betrayed by one whom he called his disciple? Surely if he was God he would not have needed to flee, or been taken away bound, and least of all to be left in the lurch and deserted by his companions, who shared everything with him personally, considered him their teacher.

Nonetheless, Judas is after all listed in each list of the Twelve in the Gospels (Matt. 10:4; Mark 3:19; Luke 6:16). His credentials are solid!

The question of his being in the Twelve has less to do with Judas than with whether Jesus ever really created an inner circle of disciples consisting of precisely twelve persons. The number twelve used of the inner circle seems to have come from the twelve tribes of Israel. One can detect the beginnings of such an idea at the conclusion of the Sayings Gospel Q (Q 22:28, 30):

You who have followed me will sit on thrones judging the twelve tribes of Israel.

Then Matthew edited this conclusion of Q to suggest that, since a disciple of Jesus was judging each of the twelve tribes, there would surely be twelve judgment seats (Matt. 20:28):

. . . you who have followed me will also sit on twelve thrones, judging the twelve tribes of Israel.

Here the idea of judging the twelve tribes of Israel clearly preceded the idea of there being twelve thrones, which in turn would engender the idea of twelve members of the inner circle. So one may assume that they arrived at the number twelve not by counting those in the inner circle, but by counting tribes. In fact, Paul can simply refer to the Twelve, on an occasion when in fact no more than eleven could have been involved. For example, in the list of resurrection appearances, Paul lists (1 Cor. 15:5):

. . . he appeared to Cephas, then to the twelve.

But at the time of the resurrection appearances, Judas was no longer a member of the Twelve. At most, Jesus appeared to eleven. But Paul's point is only that Jesus appeared to the inner circle of disciples, which was named the Twelve. In fact, some of the persons named in the Twelve are names only—their names never crop up in specific stories. Names that usually crop up together in stories of the inner circle are Peter, James, and John.

A Jewish-Christian Gospel that did not gain admission into the New Testament, the Gospel of the Ebionites, listed only nine disciples, including Judas, but in the calling of Matthew it referred to there being "twelve apostles as a witness to Israel." Here again the association with the twelve tribes of Israel is implied.

Irrespective of whether the Twelve was an actual number of members in the inner circle during Jesus's public ministry, it seems clear that Judas was a member of that inner circle. His name would hardly have been inserted into the list later, after he had given Jesus over and committed suicide. But what can we know about him?

WHAT DID JUDAS ACTUALLY DO?

The Gospel of John presents Judas as the treasurer of the Jesus movement, as a way to discredit him in the story of Mary and Martha (John 12:4–6):

But Judas Iscariot, one of his disciples (the one who was about to give him over), said, "Why was this perfume not sold for three hundred denarii and the money given to the

whom I give this piece of bread when I have dipped it in the dish." So when he had dipped the piece of bread, he gave it to Judas son of Simon Iscariot. After he received the piece of bread, Satan entered into him. Jesus said to him, "Do quickly what you are going to do." . . . So, after receiving the piece of bread, he immediately went out. And it was night.

What then is so terribly wrong with what Judas left the upper room to do, namely to give Jesus over to the Jewish authorities? After all, he was even fulfilling the prophecy of the Hebrew scriptures! And he was just obeying orders: "Do quickly what you are going to do."

All of this sounds much more like what the learned Evangelists could compose, with the help of the Hebrew scriptures in front of them (in Greek translation), than like an actual dialogue in the upper room at the Last Supper, where literacy was at a much lower level!

DID JUDAS ISCARIOT "BETRAY" JESUS?

The Gospel of Mark presents in graphic detail the scene in the Garden of Gethsemane, where Judas plays the central role (Mark 14:43–45):

And immediately, while he was still speaking, Judas came, one of the twelve, and with him a crowd with swords and clubs, from the chief priests and the scribes and the elders. Now the one who turned him over had given them a sign, saying, "The one I shall kiss is the man; seize him and lead him away under guard." And when he came, he went up to him at once, and said, "Master!" And he kissed him. And they laid hands on him and seized him.

What is actually going on here in the case of Judas? Several recent books about Judas have turned a sympathetic ear to him, sensing that what he is reported to have done was not all that wrong, after all. The more fictional presentation of Ray Anderson presents a dialogue between Jesus and Judas in which Jesus forgives Judas—and his book already bore the title *The Gospel according to Judas!*[2] Hans-Josef Klauck, a German professor who has recently joined the faculty of the University of Chicago's Divinity School, laid out a very balanced assessment of Judas as "a disciple of the Lord," in a work that unfortunately is available only in German.[3] William Klassen's book *Judas: Betrayer or Friend of Jesus?*[4] defends the thesis that Judas was indeed more friend than betrayer. And Kim Paffenroth, who specializes in the area of religion and film, has a very sympathetic though half-fictional presentation in *Judas: Images of the Lost Disciple.*[5]

The thesis of Klassen's book is that Judas did not *betray* Jesus, but only *gave* him *over* to the appropriate Jewish authorities to evaluate his claims, a quite appropriate and understandable transaction within the Judaism of that day. Hence we are wrong to understand Judas as a *traitor*, as if what the Gospels present him doing is a *betrayal*. Klassen points out:[6]

> Not one ancient classical Greek text . . . has the connotation of treachery. Any lexicon that suggests otherwise is guilty of theologizing rather than assisting us to find the meaning of Greek words through usage.

Hence, the Greek word in the Gospels that is translated as "betray" (*paradidomi*) does not actually have that basically negative meaning that we associate with betrayal in English.

In the standard Greek-English dictionary of the New Testament that all scholars use,[7] the first meaning is listed neutrally as "hand over, turn over, give up" a person. But it has also the decidedly positive meaning "give over, commend, commit," for example, to commend a person "to the grace of God" (Acts 14:26; 15:40). It often means "hand down, pass on, transmit, relate, teach" the oral or written tradition. It is in fact most familiar to us in the liturgy of the Lord's Supper, "For I received from the Lord what I also *handed on* to you" (1 Cor. 11:23), and in the way Paul introduced a list of resurrection appearances: "For I *handed on* to you as of first importance what I in turn had received" (1 Cor. 15:3). It is consistent with this double meaning of the verb that the noun means a *handing over* or a *handing down* both in the sense of an *arrest* and in the sense of the *transmission* of *tradition*. It is clear from the use of this verb that Judas *handed* Jesus *over*. The etymology of the Greek word is neutrally *give over*, which I hence use in what follows. But what that *giving over* actually meant is the question at issue.

In the whole of the New Testament, the literal term *traitor* is applied to Judas Iscariot only once, in Luke's naming him as the last in the list of the Twelve (Luke 6:16): "Judas Iscariot, who became a traitor." Is this a mistake on Luke's part?

JUDAS ISCARIOT GAVE JESUS OVER TO THE JEWISH AUTHORITIES

There have been a lot of efforts to define in theological detail what it was that Judas "betrayed" about Jesus, such as the fact that Jesus was the Messiah. But the record is clear in this regard: Judas did not reveal anything about who Jesus was or what he taught or did. Judas simply revealed where Jesus was. Mark makes this quite clear (Mark 14:1–2):

> It was now two days before the Passover and the feast of Unleavened Bread. And the chief priests and the scribes were seeking how to arrest him by stealth, and kill him;

for they said, Not during the feast, lest there be a tumult of the people.

This in turn is a flashback to an earlier comment at the cleansing of the Temple (Mark 11:18–19):

And when the chief priests and the scribes heard it, they kept looking for a way to kill him; for they were afraid of him, because the whole crowd was spellbound by his teaching. And when evening came, Jesus and his disciples went out of the city.

Klassen's main point is that for Judas to turn Jesus in to the proper Jewish authorities is not necessarily a hostile "betrayal," but rather a proper procedure in the Jewish world of the day. He comes to the following conclusion:[8]

What precisely was Judas's contribution? I submit that in the grand scheme of things, it was quite modest. In discussions with Jesus, he had often heard Jesus criticize the Temple hierarchy. When Judas reminded Jesus that his own advice had always been to rebuke the sinner directly, Jesus may have said that an occasion to confront the high priest directly had not appeared. Perhaps at that point Judas offered to arrange it, hoping that the process of rebuke would work. At the same time, he may have questioned Jesus about his own faithfulness to his mission. All of this could have led to a plan whereby Judas would arrange a meeting with Jesus and the high priests, each agreeing to that meeting on their own terms and with their own hopes for the outcome. This role in the "handing over" was later transformed into a more sinister one, especially after Judas died at his own hand. Whether the reader is able to accept this interpretation of the earliest tradition available to us, I submit that it is at least as plausible as the very negative view of Judas that still pervades the church but rests on a very shaky foundation.

This alternative is of course fleshed out with undocumented speculation about what might have gone on between Jesus and Judas, and therefore is hardly a convincing argument. Yet it does illustrate the other alternative to the standard view, that Judas was radically disloyal and simply *betrayed* Jesus. And it does show how *The Gospel of Judas* could, without too much fantasy, have made Judas into the hero of the story.

THE SUICIDE OF JUDAS

Whereas the Gospel of Mark reports nothing more specific about Judas's fate than Jesus pronouncing woe on the one who turns him in (Mark 14:21), Matthew proceeds to describe in some detail Judas's remorse and suicide (Matt. 27:3–10):

When Judas, the one turning him in, saw that Jesus was condemned, he changed his mind and brought back the thirty pieces of silver to the chief priests and the elders. He said, "I have sinned by giving over innocent blood." But they said, "What is that to us? See to it yourself." Throwing down the pieces of silver in the temple, he departed; and he went and hanged himself. But the chief priests, taking the pieces of silver, said, "It is not lawful to put them into the treasury, since they are blood money." After conferring together, they used them to buy the potter's field as a place to bury foreigners. For this reason that field has been called the Field of Blood to this day. Then was fulfilled what had been spoken through the prophet Jeremiah, And they took the thirty pieces of silver, the price of the one on whom a price had been set, on whom

some of the people of Israel had set a price, and they gave
them for the potter's field, as the Lord commanded me."[9]

Rather than this story being a strikingly exact fulfillment of a
prophecy from the Old Testament, it is, like several other details
in the passion narrative, more likely to be the other way around:
the prophecy engendered the detail in the story. The Old Testament was considered a thoroughly reliable source for facts fulfilled by Jesus. One need only read Zechariah 11:12–13:

> Then I said to them, If it seems right to you, give me my
> wages; but if not, keep them. So they weighed out as my
> wages thirty shekels of silver. The Lord said to me, Throw
> it into the treasury—this lordly price at which I was val-
> ued by them. So I took the thirty shekels of silver and
> threw them into the treasury in the house of the Lord.

For example, the detail that those who crucified Jesus "divided his clothes among them, casting lots to decide what each
should take" (Mark 15:25), comes from Psalm 22:18:

> They divided my clothes among themselves, and for my
> clothing they cast lots.

Such details from the crucifixion story probably do not reflect
eyewitness reports. But only in modern times have historians
changed their methods enough to question the factuality of
details derived only from Old Testament quotations.

Luke also writes that Judas committed suicide, in a report
that diverges slightly from that of Matthew (Acts 1:15–19):

> In those days Peter stood up among the believers (togeth-
> er the crowd numbered about one hundred twenty persons)
> and said, "Friends, the scripture had to be fulfilled, which

the Holy Spirit through David foretold concerning Judas, who became a guide for those who arrested Jesus—for he was numbered among us and was allotted his share in this ministry." (Now this man acquired a field with the reward of his wickedness; and falling headlong, he burst open in the middle and all his bowels gushed out. This became known to all the residents of Jerusalem, so that the field was called in their language *Hakeldama,* that is, Field of blood.)

These two narratives of Judas's suicide would seem to confirm the fact that he did indeed commit suicide, though the specifics of the two stories are mutually exclusive. In Matthew, he hangs himself, in Acts, he falls forward and ruptures himself. Both reports associate the suicide (in different ways) with the place name "field of blood" purchased with the thirty pieces of silver, but in one instance it is purchased by the Jewish authorities with the money he threw back at them (Matt. 27:5–7), in the other it is purchased by Judas himself with the money he was given, to become the place where he killed himself (Acts 1:18). Since the details are mutually exclusive, one is hardly copying the other. Rather, we should assume that they share a tradition with the overlapping facts that Judas committed suicide and that the term "field of blood" is in some way associated with his suicide.

THE REHABILITATION OF JUDAS ISCARIOT

No one in our history has such a bad name as Judas Iscariot. You only have to sneer "Judas!" or say "thirty pieces of silver" or "Judas kiss" to score your put-down, without going into detail. People who have never read the Gospels know what you mean! It is like referring to someone who betrays one's country as a "Benedict Arnold," without needing to know any details of his betrayal of the American colonies to the British.

Maybe Judas Iscariot needs to be rehabilitated! After all, the Evangelists presented the Twelve as quite dull about Jesus's mission, yet they have become honorific names used to accredit the Gospels of Matthew and John; Peter is said to have rebuked Jesus when he foretold his passion, but Peter's reputation has shifted from "Satan" to "rock"; Jesus's family tried to restrain him early in his ministry, but now it is dogma that Mary has been assumed into heaven, where she can be appealed to: "Hail, Mary, mother of God," as one recites the rosary. Thus the dubious characters in the story have all become saints—except for Judas Iscariot! Has his time not come?

I have used with much appreciation the appealing and scholarly book by the Mennonite theologian William Klassen.[10] As indicated above, he has argued convincingly that the translations *betray, betrayal,* and *traitor* are simply not what the Greek term means. Rather it means *give over, hand over, turn in.*

This neutral translation is then defended by the account itself. Jesus has been telling the Twelve again and again in great detail that he must go to Jerusalem to die, and reproached Peter for not accepting the fact: it is prophesied in the Hebrew scriptures and hence is the will of God, which Jesus must fulfill. Judas is playing an indispensable role in the divine plan, and surely must know it. He himself had been prophesied already in the Hebrew scriptures (John 13:18): "The one who ate my bread has lifted his heel against me" (Ps. 41:10). He is just doing what Jesus tells him to do (John 13:27): "Do quickly what you are going to do." What's so wrong with that?

Of course much of this is Markan theology rather than historical fact, which is sometimes overlooked in the effort to exonerate Judas. And even Mark, while fitting Judas into the plan of salvation, does actually pronounce woe on him as well (Mark 14:21). Yet, on the other hand, one notices the bad press Mark gives to the stupid Twelve, Peter (i.e. *Satan*), and the

Holy Family, who are embarrassed by the bad impression Jesus is making as a fanatic and wanting to take him home to keep him out of circulation (though his mother does stick by him on Good Friday to the bitter end, and his brother James surfaces as a leader of the Jerusalem Church). But Christianity has rehabilitated all of them, and so it is a bit inconsistent to leave Judas Iscariot on the hook!

The argument has been made that Judas may have thought that having the official Jewish authorities investigate Jesus's claims was the appropriate thing to do, for they would surely understand his message and endorse his ministry. Yet Jesus's triple prediction of the details of Good Friday in Mark refers explicitly to "the chief priests and the scribes" as perpetrators of the evil, so that Judas would have been the most stupid of the Twelve not to know what would happen if he gave Jesus over to them. It is very difficult to interpret the canonical Gospels as being on Judas's side. Matthew and Luke do not really clean up Mark's story to exonerate Judas, and the Gospel of John is the worst of all. To be sure, Matthew and the book of Acts report Judas's remorse, hurling back the thirty pieces of silver to the Jewish authorities or buying a place to commit suicide, and then taking his own life. Does this not help some to exonerate him?

Perhaps the most fruitful way to go at giving Judas a better place in our minds and hearts is to recall what Jesus himself said about forgiveness. Not only is there the comment about those who were doing him in: "Forgive them, for they know not what they do" (emulated by the first Christian martyr, Stephen, at his stoning, Acts 7:60). And not only did he tell one of the criminals being crucified with him (Luke 23:43): "Today you will be with me in Paradise." His own teachings pointed in the same way, in saying after saying, many of which we venerate as the Sermon on the Mount (Q 6:27–38; Q 15:4–5,7; 15:8–10; 17:3–4):

Love your enemies and pray for those persecuting you, so that you may become sons of your Father, for he raises his sun on bad and good and rains on the just and unjust.

The one who slaps you on the cheek, offer him the other as well; and to the person wanting to take you to court and get your shirt, turn over to him the coat as well. And the one who conscripts you for one mile, go with him a second. To the one who asks of you, give; and from the one who borrows, do not ask back what is yours.

And the way you want people to treat you, that is how you treat them.

If you love those loving you, what reward do you have? Do not even tax collectors do the same? And if you lend to those from whom you hope to receive, what reward do you have? Do not even the Gentiles do the same?

Be full of pity, just as your Father is full of pity.

Do not pass judgment, so you are not judged. For with what judgment you pass judgment, you will be judged. And with the measurement you use to measure out, it will be measured out to you.

Which person is there among you who has a hundred sheep, on losing one of them, will not leave the ninety-nine in the mountains and go hunt for the lost one? And if it should happen that he finds it, I say to you that he rejoices over it more than over the ninety-nine that did not go astray.

Or what woman who has ten coins, if she were to lose one coin, would not light a lamp and sweep the house and hunt until she finds? And on finding she calls the friends and neighbors, saying: Rejoice with me, for I found the coin which I had lost. Just so, I tell you, there is joy before the angels over one repenting sinner.

If your brother sins against you, rebuke him; and if he repents, forgive him. And if seven times a day he sins against you, also seven times shall you forgive him.

So should we forgive Judas? Love our enemy? I do not think the efforts to argue that what he did was the right thing to do under the circumstances have proven their case. But I do think we can stop using him as a whipping boy, and seek a fairer, more forgiving relation to him.

THREE

The Gnostic Judas

The first thing we hear about Judas after the New Testament is—his vindication! In the middle of the second century, a *Gospel of Judas* was written by a Gnostic sect called Cainites. Of course it was promptly suppressed, but apparently it is this same document that has been rediscovered in our own time. But what did we already know about *The Gospel of Judas* from the heresy-hunting church fathers who condemned it, and from what we know about how books were written back then?

The Gospel of Judas is first mentioned by Irenaeus. He wrote his *Refutation of All Heresies* in Lyon, France, around 180 CE. It is then documented by another heresy-hunter, Epiphanius, Bishop of Salamis on the island of Cyprus, in the fourth century. So we have to begin with them.

The horrified report by Irenaeus tells us a good deal of what we know about how the Cainites used the Bible, and hence how they would interpret the biblical accounts of Judas. In fact, Irenaeus actually mentions *The Gospel of Judas* in that connection:[1]

[Some] declare that Cain derived his being from the Power above, and acknowledge that Esau, Korah, the Sodomites, and all such persons, are related to themselves. On this account, they add, they have been assailed by the Creator, yet no one of them has suffered injury. For Sophia was in the habit of carrying off what belongs to her from them to herself. They declare that Judas the traitor was thoroughly acquainted with these things, and that he alone, knowing the truth as no others did, accomplished the mystery of the betrayal; by him all things, both earthly and heavenly, were thus thrown into confusion. They produce a fabricated work to this effect, which they entitle *The Gospel of Judas.*

Esau, Korah, and the Sodomites are of course very bad company for Cain to keep! And we know a person by the company he keeps! Judas's associates were so terrible that the God of the Hebrew scriptures punished them severely. Let's look at the specifics:

Esau is the older son of Isaac and Rebecca, who sold his birthright for a "mess of pottage" to his younger brother Jacob. As Paul summarizes it (Rom. 9:13):

As it is written,
  I have loved Jacob,
  But I have hated Esau.

Or, as Hebrews puts it (Heb. 12:16):

See to it that no one becomes like Esau, an immoral and godless person, who sold his birthright for a single meal.

Korah was of course the son of Esau (Gen. 36:5, 14; 1 Chron. 1:35), if not his grandson (Gen. 36:16). Perhaps it is basically the name of a clan. But in any case Korah is given credit/blame for instigating a revolt against Moses and Aaron, about which we will hear more later.

The Sodomites? This is the name about which you may already be best informed, if you know what is named after them: sodomy.

Sodom was a large city at the southern end of the Dead Sea that already in antiquity was a notorious ruin. I participated in the archeological excavation of the most probable site, Bab ed-Dhra, back in 1965, though we found no incriminating evidence, of course.

Abraham's nephew Lot lived there. He extended oriental hospitality to two angels as house guests. But before bedtime, things suddenly took a turn for the worse (Gen. 19:4–5):

> But before they lay down, the men of the city, the men of Sodom, both young and old, all the people to the last man, surrounded the house; and they called to Lot, Where are the men who came to you tonight? Bring them out to us, so that we may know them.

God's destruction of Sodom was notorious already in antiquity, as a warning against committing abominations deserving equal or worse punishment (Q 10:12):

> For Sodom it shall be more bearable on that day than for that town.

Sodom, along with its sister-city Gomorrah, went down in history as the worst city of antiquity. As a result, their punishment was legendary (Rom. 9:29):

> And as Isaiah predicted,
>> If the Lord of hosts had not left survivors to us,
>> We would have fared like Sodom
>> And been made like Gomorrah.

Their condemnation continued even more explicitly in the post-apostolic age (Jude 7):

Likewise, Sodom and Gomorrah and the surrounding cities, which in the same manner as they, indulged in sexual immorality and went after other flesh, serve as an example by undergoing a punishment of eternal fire.

Then, in what is probably the last New Testament book to be written, as late as the second century, one gets the fullest formulation of their depravity (2 Pet. 2:4, 6, 9–10):

For if God did not spare the angels when they sinned, but cast them into hell and committed them to chains of deepest darkness to be kept until the judgment; . . . and if by turning the cities of Sodom and Gomorrah to ashes he condemned them to extinction and made them an example of what is coming to the ungodly; . . . then the Lord knows how to rescue the godly from trial, and to keep the unrighteous under punishment until the day of judgment—especially those who indulge their flesh in depraved lust, and who despise authority.

This then is the Sodom that Irenaeus puts in association with Cain!

Two centuries after Irenaeus, Epiphanius also quotes and refutes the Gnostic sect that produced *The Gospel of Judas:*[2]

And others say, "No, he [Judas] betrayed him despite his goodness because of heavenly knowledge. For the [evil] archons knew, they say, "that the weaker power would be drained if Christ were given over to crucifixion." "And when Judas found this out," they say, "he was anxious, and did all he could to betray him, and performed a good work for our salvation. And we must commend him and give him the credit, since the salvation of the cross was effected for us through him, and the revelation of the things which that occasioned."

Hence Judas did not betray the Savior from knowledge, as these people say; nor will the Jews be rewarded for crucifying the Lord, though we certainly have salvation through the cross. Judas did not betray him to make him the saving of us, but from the ignorance, envy and greed of the denial of God.

"And therefore," they say, "Judas has found out all about them [the higher powers]." For they claim him as kin too and consider him particularly knowledgeable, so that they even attribute a short work to him, which they call *The Gospel of Judas*.

Here, Epiphanius is relating a very familiar Gnostic dualism about this world being evil and the heavenly world being good, so the death of Christ's weaker, earthly body could have been seen by Judas as the necessary event to release Christ's heavenly nature. Epiphanius condemns any notion of Judas as being motivated by anything other than ignorance and greed, but acknowledges that there are some, to the contrary, who commend Judas as "knowledgeable" (the Gnostic's essential theme), give him some credit for Christ's salvific act, and attribute a gospel to him.

WHAT SCHOLARS ALREADY KNOW ABOUT *THE GOSPEL OF JUDAS*

There is a standard scholarly reference work about such Gospels that were not accepted into the canon of the New Testament. It reports, in all too academic a way, but nonetheless succinctly and exhaustively, all that has been known thus far about the Cainites and their *Gospel of Judas*. Let me quote this reference work, with all due apologies for its pedantry:[3]

1. **Attestation:** the most important and oldest source here is Irenaeus (*adv. Haer.* I 31.1 = Theodoret of Cyrus, *Haereticorum fabularum compendium* I 15, PG LXXXIII 368 B): certain gnostic sectaries possessed in addition to other works of their own composition, a 'gospel' under the name of the traitor Judas (*Judae euangelium*, . . .); these sectaries are elsewhere identified with the Cainites, and reckoned among the 'Gnostics' of Epiphanius, the Nicolaitans, Ophites, Sethians, or Carpocratians. The existence and title of the document . . . are also attested by Epiphanius (*Pan.* 38.1.5; II, 63.13f. Holl.)

2. **Content:** it would be rash to ascribe to the Gospel of Judas a quotation derived by Epiphanius from a Cainite book (*Pan.* 38.2.4; II, 64.17–19 Holl. 'This is the angel who blinded Moses, and these are the angels who hid the people about Korah and Dathan and Abiram, and carried them off'). Still less reason is there for ascribing to this gospel a formula reproduced by Irenaeus (I 31.2 and Epiphanius 38.2.2), which accompanied the sexual rite practiced by the sect for the attainment of the 'perfect gnosis.' As to the subject and content of the apocryphon, we are reduced to simple conjecture, supported at best by some characteristics of Cainite doctrine as it is known from the notices of the heresiologues. It is possible, but far from certain, that this 'gospel' contained a passion story setting forth the 'mystery of the betrayal' (*proditionis mysterium*, . . .) and explaining how Judas by his treachery made possible the salvation of all mankind: either he forestalled the destruction of the truth proclaimed by Christ, or he thwarted the designs of the evil powers, the archons, who wished to

prevent the crucifixion since they knew that it would deprive them of their feeble power and bring salvation to men (ps.-Tertullian, *adv. Omn. Haer.* 2; Epiphanius, *Pan.* 38.3.3–5; Filastrius, *Haer.* 34; Augustine, *de Haer.* 18; ps.-Jerome, *Indiculus de haer.* 8; cf. Bauer, *Leben Jesu*, p. 176). However that may be, the work was probably in substance an exposition of the secret doctrine (licentious and violently antinomian in character) ostensibly revealed by Judas, a summary of the Truth or of the superior and perfect Gnosis which he was supposed to possess by virtue of a revelation (Irenaeus, I 31.1; Epiph. *Pan.* 38.1.5; Filastrius, *Haer.* 34).

3. **Dating:** *The Gospel of Judas* was of course composed before 180, the date at which it is mentioned for the first time by Irenaeus in *adv. Haer.* If it is in fact a Cainite work, and if this sect—assuming that it was an independent Gnostic group—was constituted in part, as has sometimes been asserted, in dependence on the doctrine of Marcion, the apocryphon can scarcely have been composed before the middle of the 2nd century. This would, however, be to build on weak arguments. At most we may be inclined to suspect a date between 130 and 170 or thereabouts.

Very little is actually known about *The Gospel of Judas.* But more can be known about the sect that is said to have produced the text, the Cainites. Irenaeus classified them as Gnostics, and Epiphanius associated them with "the people about Korah and Dathan and Abiram." This is of course guilt by association. But at least it shows how they were seen by the early church fathers.

What had Dathan and Abiram done that was so terrible? The Hebrew scriptures tell the story in all its gory details (Num. 16:27–33):

Dathan and Abiram came out and stood at the entrance of their tents, together with their wives, their children, and their little ones. And Moses said, This is how you shall know that the Lord has sent me to do all these works; it has not been of my own accord: If these people die a natural death, or if a natural fate comes on them, then the Lord has not sent me. But if the Lord creates something new, and the ground opens its mouth and swallows them up, with all that belongs to them, and they go down alive into Sheol, then you shall know that these men have despised the Lord. As soon as he finished speaking all these words, the ground under them was split apart. The earth opened its mouth and swallowed them up, along with their households—everyone who belonged to Korah and all their goods. So they with all that belonged to them went down alive into Sheol; the earth closed over them, and they perished from the midst of the assembly.

The story is told again in a simple listing of the Israelites who came out of Egypt with Moses (Num. 26:9–11):

The descendants of Eliab: Nemuel, Dathan, and Abiram. These are the same Dathan and Abiram, chosen from the congregation, who rebelled against Moses and Aaron in the company of Korah, when they rebelled against the Lord, and the earth opened its mouth and swallowed them up along with Korah, when that company died, when the fire devoured two hundred fifty men; and they became a warning. Notwithstanding, the sons of Korah did not die.

Even when Deuteronomy summarizes what God had done for the chosen people, this has to be repeated (Deut. 11:2, 6–7):

Remember today that . . . it is you who must acknowledge his greatness, his mighty hand and his outstretched arm, . . . what he did to Dathan and Abiram, sons of Eliab son of Reuben, how in the midst of all Israel the earth opened its mouth and swallowed them up, along with their households, their tents, and every living being in their company.

A psalm recalls (Ps. 106:7, 16–18):

Our ancestors, when they were in Egypt, did not consider your wonderful works; they did not remember the abundance of your steadfast love, but rebelled against the Most High at the Red Sea. . . . They were jealous of Moses in the camp, and of Aaron, the holy one of the Lord. The earth opened and swallowed up Dathan, and covered the faction of Abiram. Fire also broke out in their company; the flame burned up the wicked.

What these terrible people did was to seek to share with the family of Aaron the priestly function in the tabernacle. Terrible? Is it just our modern sensitivities that takes offense when God takes *credit* that 250 Israelites "go down alive into Hell," "together with their wives, their children, and their little ones"? Is that also something that could have offended readers at an earlier time, making them even wonder just how good and loving their God really was? But watch out—I may have just about talked you into becoming a Gnostic, even a Cainite!

All one has to do, or had to do back then, is to be very painfully aware of just how terrible the world really is, so terrible in many ways to be unconvinced that poor old Adam and Eve could take the blame for all of it. God must have made it that way—if not before Adam and Eve, then in any case as terrible punishment after Adam and Eve.

A GNOSTIC CREATION STORY

Is what Adam and Eve wanted to do really so terrible as to get the blame for all the evil that is in the world? A thinking person (their term: a Gnostic) could give a literal interpretation of the creation story of Genesis 3 that turns it upside down:[4]

> It is written in the Law about this: God commanded Adam, "From every tree you may eat, but from the tree that is in the middle of paradise do not eat, for on the day that you eat from it, you will certainly die." But the snake was wiser than all the other animals in paradise, and he persuaded Eve by saying, "On the day that you eat from the tree that is in the middle of paradise, the eyes of your mind will be opened." Eve obeyed; she stretched out her hand, took from the tree, and ate. She also gave some fruit to her husband who was with her. Immediately they realized that they were naked. They took some fig leaves and put them on as aprons.
>
> But at evening time God came along, walking in the middle of paradise. When Adam saw him, he went into hiding. And God said, "Adam, where are you?" He answered, "I have come under the fig tree." At that very moment God realized that he had eaten from the tree about which he had commanded him, "Don't eat from it."
>
> And God said, "Who is it who instructed you?" Adam answered, "The woman you gave me." And the woman said, "It is the snake who instructed me." He cursed the snake and called him Devil. And God said, "Look, Adam has become like one of us now that he knows evil and good." Then he said, "Let's throw him out of paradise so he doesn't take from the tree of life, eat, and live forever."
>
> What kind of a God is this? First, he begrudged Adam's eating from the tree of knowledge. Second, he said,

"Adam, where are you?" God does not have foreknowl-
edge; otherwise, wouldn't he have known from the beginning? He has certainly shown himself to be a malicious
grudger. And what kind of a god is this?

Great is the blindness of those who read such things,
and they don't know him. He said, "I am the jealous God;
I will bring the sins of the fathers upon the children up
to three and four generations." He also said, "I will make
their heart thick, and I will cause their minds to become
blind, that they might not understand nor comprehend
the things that are said." But these are things he says to
those who believe in him and worship him!

The Gnostic would ask of us, Are you also the victim of blindness, not knowing that God is a jealous God, making your
heart thick, your mind blind, so that you will not understand?
Don't you realize that God himself is not all that smart, not
even knowing where Adam is? What's wrong with the eyes of
your mind being opened? What's wrong with Adam becoming like "one of us," like a divine being, godlike? What's so
wrong with eating from the tree of life and living forever? Are
you really against the immortality of the soul? What kind of
God is this, after all—"a malicious grudger"? A malevolent
God like that would surely explain how the world he created
is so terrible.

Is that really the last word? Isn't there some hope somewhere? Maybe high above the heavens—the same evil God
who made the earth also made the heavens—and so, *beyond*
the heavens? Some really decent, good, loving God that the
Hebrew scriptures don't know about, a hidden God? Yet a hidden God who did reveal himself, on rare occasions, to persons
who resisted the evil God, and hence got punished by the evil
God, and got a terrible reputation in the scriptures dictated by
the evil God?

THE MALIGNED CAIN

Who got worse notoriety in the scriptures than Cain? Just listen (Gen. 4:1–15):

> Now the man knew his wife Eve, and she conceived and bore Cain, saying, "I have produced a man with the help of the Lord." Next she bore his brother Abel. Now Abel was a keeper of sheep, and Cain a tiller of the ground. In the course of time Cain brought to the Lord an offering of the fruit of the ground, and Abel for his part brought of the firstlings of his flock, their fat portions. And the Lord had regard for Abel and his offering, but for Cain and his offering he had no regard. So Cain was very angry, and his countenance fell. The Lord said to Cain, "Why are you angry, and why has your countenance fallen? If you do well, will you not be accepted? And if you do not do well, sin is lurking at the door; its desire is for you, but you must master it."
>
> Cain said to his brother Abel, "Let us go out to the field." And when they were in the field, Cain rose up against his brother Abel, and killed him. Then the Lord said to Cain, "Where is your brother Abel?" He said, "I do not know; am I my brother's keeper?" And the Lord said, "What have you done? Listen, your brother's blood is crying out to me from the ground! And now you are cursed from the ground, which has opened its mouth to receive your brother's blood from your hand. When you till the ground, it will no longer yield to you its strength; you will be a fugitive and a wanderer on the earth."
>
> Cain said to the Lord, "My punishment is greater than I can bear! Today you have driven me away from the soil, and I shall be hidden from your face; I shall be a fugitive and a wanderer on the earth, and anyone who meets me

may kill me." Then the Lord said to him, "Not so! Whoever kills Cain will suffer a sevenfold vengeance. And the Lord put a mark on Cain, so that no one who came upon him would kill him."

What kind of a God is that, who even back at the beginning of the story rejects the farmer's offering, even though it is all the farmer has produced that he could offer? Cain may have overreacted, but did not God also overreact—condemning Cain to be a fugitive and a wanderer on the earth, no longer able to make a livelihood out of farming? And, would you like to walk around the rest of your life with the "mark of Cain" on you, whatever that was?

Cain, who gets overly punished by a vengeful God, is a precurser of Korah, Dathan, and Abiram, who suffered such a terrible fate along with their families, simply because they wanted a more important role in worshiping God in the temple. They get the bad press, whereas their opponents, Moses and his brother Aaron, stay in power. But is that then really the last word? The Cainites might well have taken hope for, after all: "The sons of Korah did not die!"

The Gnostics might well have said: We who are in the know, who think for ourselves and see through the sham, have been enlightened by a hidden God far above, who is free of all this impossible system under which the world suffers. This hidden God frees us, he does not enslave us!

And if you read not only the Hebrew scriptures with these glasses on, but also read the Christian scriptures this way, whom do you light upon as the defamed hero that is damned for doing the only decent thing, namely seeing to it that prophecy is fulfilled, God's will done, Jesus obeyed, and thus humanity saved? Well, Judas, of course! Maybe the Gospels of Matthew, Mark, Luke, and John need to be replaced by—*The Gospel of Judas*?

We will see . . .

HOW TO MAKE A PAPYRUS BOOK

We know that *The Gospel of Judas* is from an early papyrus codex. The Nag Hammadi Codices are in this regard very similar—both discoveries in Middle and Upper Egypt are of third- and fourth-century papyrus codices with Coptic translations of Gnostic tractates originally composed in Greek. Since I worked intensively for years restoring and publishing for UNESCO the Nag Hammadi Codices,[5] I do know a lot about the kind of book that contains *The Gospel of Judas*.[6] So let me tell you about how papyrus books were made in antiquity, both the original second-century Greek book containing *The Gospel of Judas* and the third- or fourth-century Coptic copy that has now surfaced.

Papyrus is a plant that grew in antiquity in the shallow waters of the Nile River. It produced a long stalk that was cut and peeled, and then its pith cut into thin strips. These strips were laid vertically side by side on a flat surface, and then a second layer of strips was rowed up on top horizontally. This was then pressed together, indeed pounded, until the juice in the pith formed a kind of glue that held both layers together as a flat surface on which one could write. One such writing surface could be as long as six feet, to judge by those whose length I calculated in the process of conserving the Nag Hammadi Codices. At the end of such a piece of papyrus, one could paste another, with an overlap of about half an inch where they were pasted together. One could proceed in this way, piece after piece, to produce as long a writing surface as one wished.

People back then wrote on the surface with the horizontal fibers, since one wrote horizontally and thus with the flow of the fibers, rather than having to bump across from fiber to fiber going against the grain. One wrote in columns about the width of a column in a book today, then left a space of an inch or so, and then wrote the next column, and so on, for as long a book as one wished. Then one rolled up the long papyrus strip into a roll, with the writing surface protected by being on the inside, and *voila!* there you have a papyrus scroll!

A rolled-up scroll would be hard to identify, especially if one had more than one lying side by side. So on the outside, at the end that was visible when the scroll was rolled up, one wrote some identifying phrase, at right angles to the text on the inside, so as still to be writing in the direction of the fibers, for on the outside these were in the opposite direction to the fibers on the inside. This is the origin of what we would think of as a book "title." It may not have been chosen by the person who wrote the text of the book itself, but probably by the copyist, or the person who needed to distinguish this scroll from other scrolls. The original author would tend to suggest in the body of the text itself, at its beginning or ending (or both), the gist of what the book was all about. Sometimes it would be this that the later scribe would summarize as the label on the outside of the scroll.

These papyrus scrolls had been used for thousands of years (literally!) by the time Christianity began. But technology was advancing, and scrolls were, after all, rather cumbersome. Rolling and unrolling a scroll every time you want to put it away and then resume reading the next time was a time-consuming chore. And rolling and unrolling was hard on the papyrus, durable though it was.

About the time of the beginning of Christianity, people had developed a kind of notebook for schoolchildren, first attested in Rome: two thin small planks of wood were each lined on one side with wax, then laid together with the wax surfaces on the inside, to protect them. The schoolchild would write on the wax surfaces, then scrape it clean and write again and again, adding overnight new wax to keep it ready for use. (I remember as a child having my own small blackboard and chalk for the same purpose!)

Then it occurred to them that they could replace the wax between the planks with a few leaves of papyrus to write on. The leaves were then attached together, and to the wooden planks, so they would not fall out and get lost. The boards developed into leather covers, the few papyrus sheets became quires, and there you have something that is like a modern book: pages you can turn! They called it a *codex*, plural *codices*, to distinguish them from scrolls. That just meant a "fistfull," a book you could hold in your fist and turn pages as you read, rather than a long thing to lay out on a table and unwind with both hands.

Bit by bit books that had been composed to fit the length of a not-too-long scroll were copied into codices. Usually a scroll had to be relatively short, so that one did not have to scroll and scroll endlessly to find one's place. But a codex was easier to use—one could simply open it in the middle and go on reading where one had left off, especially since one usually numbered the pages. So several scrolls could be copied into one codex.

That is why the "books" of the Bible can become one book, the Bible—they had been written on separate scrolls (which is still today the preferred Jewish form of book for their scriptures). Now they could be copied into a single codex! This is why we have the habit of talking about the "books" of the Bible—they were originally composed each as a book in its own right, though in the Bible they are really just the length of what we might call chapters, or, as we call them in the case of the Nag Hammadi Codices, "tractates." This is also the case with the newly discovered copy of *The Gospel of Judas*, since early reports are to the effect that it is in a codex that also included at least two other texts, of which there are parallel copies in the Nag Hammadi Codices. And one may recall that Epiphanius referred to it as "a short work."

The phrase that had been put on the outside of a roll to identify what text was inside could be carried over to the codex.

When a number of "books" or tractates are included in a single codex, they need to be distinguished one from the other. That identifying phrase would be copied at the beginning or end (or both) of a text, set off by blank space and hatch-marks as decoration, as a superscript and/or subscript title.

You can see what I mean by "hatch-marks," by looking at the photograph facing the first page of the Preface of the book in your hands, at the end of the last line of the text of *The Gospel of Judas*, as well as on the otherwise blank line between the end of the text and the subscript title.

"GOSPELS" AND THEIR "AUTHORS"

Since the author of the individual book was usually not the person who wrote the label on the outside of the scroll or the title that was set off at the beginning and/or end of a tractate in a codex, there is often a slight discrepancy between the text of the tractate itself and its secondarily attached title. This is even the case with the four "Gospels" in the New Testament. Their titles inform us that they are the Gospels according to Matthew, Mark, Luke, and John. But the body of the texts of these four tractates are all anonymous. In John 21:24 we are told that the beloved disciple wrote the tractate, which is why we are sure John wrote it—until we notice that the beloved disciple is never identified as John. In fact, John is never mentioned in the Gospel of John!

There may be reasons why a Gospel was associated with a certain apostle. The calling of Levi the tax collector in Mark 2:13–17 becomes the calling of Matthew the tax collector in Matt. 9:9–13, and so, in Matthew's list of the Twelve, the apostle "Matthew" (Mark 3:18) becomes "Matthew the tax collector" (Matt. 10:3). This may have been intended as a hint by the person who wrote the Gospel, irrespective of whether it was the tax-collector Levi/Matthew or not. In any case, it would have been taken as sufficient reason to ascribe this Gospel to Matthew. But there is no place in this Gospel, or in any of the others, where the name of the Evangelist is actually said to have been the author. Rather, one now assumes that the name of the apostle to whom a Christian community appealed for its own "apostolicity" was ascribed to the Gospel that the community used and cherished as its authority. Usually by this time one no longer knew who had first composed the text.

The same situation prevails with regard to the name "Gospel" that we automatically associate with the four Gospels in the New Testament. The word *gospel* of course means "good news." Paul contrasts his *good news* with the false *good news* of his opponents, which is not to be believed, even if it comes from angels (Gal. 1:6–10). But he is not referring to a book entitled *Gospel* that he (or they) had written. In Paul's time, no Gospels had been written!

Mark's Gospel begins with the word *gospel* in the very first verse. But he is not saying that the book that follows is a Gospel, but rather that he is writing down the *good news.* Hence in Mark 1:1 *gospel* is somewhat of a mistranslation (down to and including the Revised Standard Version), or at least misleading: "The beginning of the *gospel* of Jesus Christ." The New Revised Standard Version has more correctly translated: "The beginning of the *good news* of Jesus Christ." Mark's first verse means that his whole book is the beginning of the good news that Christianity has to offer. To be sure, that use of the word *gospel* in the first verse of the oldest Gospel is no doubt the reason that copyists in later centuries used *Gospel* in the titles ascribed to each. But that means that the title *Gospel* is a creation of copyists, not of the Evangelists themselves.

When one looks at the opening of the other Gospels, we find them describing what they are doing with other nouns, indicating that they do not yet have in mind *Gospel* as the name for what they are writing. Matthew begins (Matt. 1:1): "*Book* of the genealogy of Jesus Christ." Luke bases what he is writing on records from those "compiling a *narrative*" (Luke 1:1), who were "eyewitnesses and servants of the *word*" (Luke 1:1). And at the opening of Acts, Luke refers back to his first volume, which we call the Gospel of Luke, as "the first *book*," literally "the first *word*," their way of saying Volume One, not as his "Gospel." the Gospel of John begins its Prologue with "In the beginning was the *Word*" (John 1:1). Thus they are thinking about the message, when they introduce their "Gospels." They were not aware of creating a literary genre to which their book belongs, namely: the Gospel genre.

However, the name Gospel did get attached to the four Gospels, and as they moved toward the authoritative status of being included in the New Testament, the designation Gospel could readily be attached to other writings, in an effort to accredit them as being of equal authority. But here too an examination of the body of the text of such noncanonical "Gospels" indicates that they were not called Gospels by their original authors.

This can be illustrated by the four "Gospels" to be found outside the New Testament in the Nag Hammadi Codices. The best known by far is *The Gospel of Thomas*. It exists, almost completely intact, both in a papyrus codex of the mid-fourth century in Coptic translation (Nag Hammadi Codex II, Tractate 2) and in three very fragmentary Greek vestiges from the third century (Oxyrhynchus Papyri 1, 654, and 655). Here Ralph Pöhner, in an essay entitled "Judas the Hero,"[7] quite correctly comments:

This dialogue of Jesus with Thomas counts today as very important for the history of religion: Some researchers name it "the fifth Gospel," and it could be that here even lies the original text on which the official Gospels built.

Though *The Gospel of Thomas* is less a "dialogue" than a collection of 114 sayings ascribed to Jesus, it is indeed a very important discovery, no doubt the most important Gospel outside the New Testament. It may well have older readings than the same sayings in the canonical Gospels, and in this sense be nearer to Jesus himself. In fact, I for one have made just such an argument.

Saying 36 contains at one place an older text than does the New Testament. In the familiar sayings about the ravens and lilies that demonstrate their trust in God in that they do not work (Q 12:22–31), the first instance of the lilies not working is . . . "they grow"—hardly what one would expect! But in *The Gospel of Thomas*, Saying 36 reads (in the Greek original, P.Oxy. 655): "they do not card." This is precisely the first work women did back then, in moving from the wool of the sheep to the clothing they wore. The difference in spelling is very slight. It seems probable that here *The Gospel of Thomas* has the correct text, and the New Testament has the corrupted text. I have published seven articles arguing this point alone.[8]

A further instance is the Parable of the Vineyard, which in the New Testament (Mark 12:1–12) has a secondary allegorizing interpretation imbedded in the parable itself, whereas *The Gospel of Thomas*, Saying 65, presents the original form of the parable prior to that allegorization.

But there are also sayings in *The Gospel of Thomas* that seem to presuppose the New Testament Gospels, such as Saying 16, where the number of five in the household that disagree among themselves seems based on Luke 12:52–53, though Luke seems here to have made a late addition to the Sayings Gospel Q.[9] The current scholarly view is hence that *The Gospel of Thomas* contains some material that is older than the canonical Gospels, and some material that is younger.

The idea of calling *The Gospel of Thomas* the "fifth Gospel," to which Pöhner refers with obvious approval, is in fact the title of a book I edited, though the idea was not original with me, containing a new translation of the text and an essay I wrote on the fiftieth anniversary of its discovery.[10] But that is not what the original author/collector of these 114 *sayings* ascribed to Jesus would have called his tractate.

Another instance that Pöhner lists of noncanonical Gospels is *The Gospel of Mary* (Magdalene). This is a very important second-century apocryphal Gospel, and plays an important role in the modern feminist movement. The author of this standard kind of Gnostic *dialogue* refers to them preaching the *"gospel of the kingdom,"* but also of Jesus's *words* and a *vision,* so it is not clear whether the original author chose the title *Gospel of Mary* or whether this was secondarily added. It so happens that I was the first to make *The Gospel of Mary* available in English, in *The Nag Hammadi Library in English.*[11] *The Gospel of Mary* is not among the Nag Hammadi Codices, but is found in a similar Gnostic codex, Papyrus Berolinensis 8502. Hence I thought it would be well to include it with the Nag Hammadi Codices, especially since it had been available for a long time in German but not yet in English.

I mention here such details of my involvement, not to draw attention to my work, but rather to make it clear that my criticism of Pöhner is not the standard conservative prejudice in favor of limiting oneself to the canonical Gospels to the exclusion of the noncanonical Gospels. My concern is quite the reverse: the attention we are giving to the noncanonical Gospels today should not be discredited by those who make use of this scholarly material in a nonscholarly way, such as Pöhner.

We name it *The Gospel of Thomas* because the subscript title at the end reads *The Gospel according to Thomas.* But this tractate does not tell the stories of Jesus, as do the canonical Gospels, but is limited to sayings of Jesus. This has led scholars to make a distinction between Narrative Gospels, that tell the story of Jesus (as do Matthew, Mark, Luke, and John), and Sayings

Gospels (such as the source used by Matthew and Luke called Q, and *The Gospel of Thomas*).

The Gospel of Thomas consists of 114 sayings ascribed to Jesus, each introduced with the stereotypical phrase, "Jesus says: . . ." The word *gospel* occurs nowhere in the text! Rather, sayings themselves refer to Jesus's *sayings* or *words*.

Both *saying* and *word* are translations of the same word in Coptic and Greek. It is just a distinction we make sometimes in translating. For example, where it occurred at the opening of Luke and John, we translated it *word*.

Saying 19 of *The Gospel of Thomas* reads:

> If you become disciples of mine and listen to my *sayings*, these stones will serve you.

Saying 38 reads:

> Many times you have desired to hear these *sayings*, these that I am speaking to you, and you have no one else from whom to hear them.

The opening of the text of *The Gospel of Thomas* reads: "These are the hidden *sayings* that the living Jesus spoke." The term *sayings* actually occurs in the very first saying:

> Whoever finds the interpretation of these *sayings* will not taste death.

It is clear that the author or collector of these sayings thought that the work he or she was producing was a collection of Jesus's *sayings*, not a *Gospel*.

The saying that is no doubt responsible for *The Gospel of Thomas* being ascribed to Thomas is Saying 13:

Jesus said to his disciples: "Compare me and tell me whom I am like."

Simon Peter said to him: "You are like a just messenger."

Matthew said to him: "You are like an especially wise philosopher."

Thomas said to him: "Teacher, my mouth cannot bear at all to say whom you are like."

Jesus said: "I am not your teacher. For you have drunk, you have become intoxicated at the bubbling spring that I have measured out."

And he took him, and withdrew, and he said three sayings to him.

And when Thomas came back to his companions, they asked him: "What did Jesus say to you?"

Thomas said to them: "If I tell you one of the sayings he said to me, you will pick up stones and throw them at me, and fire will come out of the stones and burn you up."

As a result of this preeminence given to Thomas, *The Gospel of Thomas* begins:

These are the hidden sayings that the living Jesus spoke, and Didymos Judas Thomas wrote them down.

And the very first saying elevates Jesus's sayings to being what actually saves:

Whoever finds the meaning of these sayings will not taste death.

From all of this it is clear that *The Gospel of Thomas* was hardly designated by its original author or compiler as a *Gospel*.

Rather he or she would have called it a collection of *sayings*. But then, in the effort to get it accredited by the church as being on a par with the *Gospels* gaining canonicity in the emerging New Testament, this collection of *sayings* of Jesus was secondarily named a *Gospel*.

The situation with another Nag Hammadi tractate, *The Gospel of Philip*, is similar. It too does not narrate the stories of Jesus, as we might expect of a Gospel, based on what is in the Gospels of the New Testament. Rather, it is engrossed in other issues, though at times referring to a saying or action of Jesus. The text never even uses the word *gospel*. However, there is one saying ascribed to Philip, which is probably why the whole text came to be ascribed to him:[12]

> Philip the apostle said: Joseph the carpenter planted a garden because he needed wood for his trade. It was he who made the cross when he planted. His offspring was Jesus and the planting was the cross.

Normally a Nag Hammadi tractate has a title separated off from the body of the text, at the top or bottom (or both), surrounded by blank papyrus and with hatch-marks to decorate it, as we have described earlier, and as you can see on the photograph opposite the Preface. But the title *The Gospel according to Philip* is jammed into the end of the last line of the text. This suggests that it was secondarily added, as a kind of afterthought, by the scribe of Nag Hammadi Codex II who copied out this tractate. It was apparently not the title intended by the anonymous author of the tractate.

In the case of *The Gospel of the Egyptians*, the situation is similar. The actual text of the tractate begins:[13] "The holy book of the Egyptians about the great invisible Spirit." And it concludes with a subscript title:[14] "The Holy Book of the Great Invisible Spirit. Amen." But then the scribe of Nag Hammadi

Codex III has inserted a note just before the subscript title, in which he writes:[15]

> *The Gospel of the Egyptians.* The God-written, holy, secret book. Grace, understanding, perception, prudence be with him who has written it, Eugnostos the beloved in the Spirit—in the flesh my name is Gongessos—and my fellow lights in incorruptibility. Jesus Christ, Son of God, Savior, ICHTHUS. God-written is the holy book of the great, invisible Spirit. Amen.

Codex III was the first codex to reach the Coptic Museum in Cairo. They were delighted to put page 69 on display, with the title *The Gospel of the Egyptians* clearly legible. So this quite secondary title has stuck with the tractate ever since! But the author of the tractate did not intend to be writing a Gospel, and his text has nothing to do either with the story or with the sayings of Jesus. The text contains the Gnostic myth of a sect that venerated Seth, the third son of Adam and Eve after Cain had killed Abel and had himself been banished (Gen. 4:25–26).

The fourth "Gospel" in the Nag Hammadi Codices is *The Gospel of Truth.* It is quite well-known, because the Jung Institute of Zürich "baptized" the codex containing it the "Jung Codex," in honor of their founding hero, the psychologist Karl Jung, who maintained that *The Gospel of Truth* made sense in the light of his psychology. They gave the tractate, which had no title of its own in the Jung Codex = Nag Hammadi Codex I, the title *The Gospel of Truth,* on the basis of the opening line:[16]

> The gospel of truth is joy for those who have received from the Father of truth the grace of knowing him.

There is apparently already an allusion to the tractate by Irenaeus. He points out that the reference in the opening of the text to this being the true gospel is a put-down for the true canonical Gospels. "Gospel of Truth" is of course not the title of the tractate, but only the author's opening blast, to refer to the message of the tractate as being the *true* gospel, in distinction from the orthodox Gospels that falsely claim to be true.

One may conclude that the title *Gospel* was not the original title of the four canonical Gospels, nor was it the original title of the four Nag Hammadi "Gospels." Both the branch of the church that was moving toward what came to be called orthodoxy, and the branch that was moving toward what came to be called heresy, designated their texts as Gospels to accredit them in the ongoing competition.

"GOSPEL"? BY "JUDAS"?

The Gospel of Judas was composed after the canonical Gospels were written, at about the same time as the Nag Hammadi Gospels were written. No doubt, like them, *The Gospel of Judas* made use of the title *Gospel* to accredit itself over against the canonical Gospels, which had secondarily popularized the title in their own quest for accreditation. As a result, we assume not only that *The Gospel of Judas* was not written by Judas—after all, he had been dead for over a century—but may not be what the public assumes a Gospel would be—a collection of the stories and/or sayings of Jesus. The four Gospels among the Nag Hammadi Codices have shown that the honorific title could be ascribed to works that we today would never call gospels, if that title had not been attached to them in the tradition. *The Gospel of Judas* will in all probability teach us a lot more about the Gnosticism of the second century than about the public ministry of Jesus, or sayings of Jesus, or Holy Week, or the like.

How has Judas been understood down through the centuries, after the New Testament presented him as giving Jesus over to the Jewish authorities, and *The Gospel of Judas* some-how vindicated him?

In antiquity, to fall on one's sword when one's leader is slain is considered a noble death. Should not Judas's suicide after Jesus's crucifixion be accorded this distinction of being a noble death? Apparently it was first Saint Augustine who decided that Judas's suicide was in fact a sin.[17] Listen to the way Augustine put it:[18]

> He did not deserve mercy; and that is why no light shone in his heart to make him hurry for pardon from the one he had betrayed.

And so, irrespective of what one might think of Judas giving Jesus over to the Jewish authorities, as implementing God's plan of salvation, or as a traitor betraying his friend, he cannot be forgiven for his suicide!

The most generous that early Christian monasticism could be to Judas was to suggest that Jesus forgave him, but ordered him to purify himself with "spiritual exercises" in the desert, such as they themselves practiced.

In the seventh century, the Bible commentator Theophylact thought Judas had not expected things to turn bad once he arranged a hearing between Jesus and the Jewish authorities, and in anguish at the outcome killed himself to "get to Hades before Jesus and thus to implore and gain salvation":[19]

> Some say that Judas, being covetous, supposed that he would make money by betraying Christ, and that Christ would not be killed but would escape from the Jews as many a time he had escaped. But when he saw him con-demned, actually already condemned to death, he repent-ed since the affair had turned out so differently from what he had expected. And so he hanged himself to get to Hades

before Jesus and thus to implore and gain salvation. Know well, however, that he put his neck into the halter and hanged himself on a certain tree, but the tree bent down and he continued to live, since it was God's will that he either be preserved for repentance or for public disgrace and shame. For they say that due to dropsy he could not pass where a wagon passed with ease; then he fell on his face and burst asunder, that is, was rent apart, as Luke says in the Acts.

A Dominican preacher, Vinzenz Ferrer, in a sermon in 1391, had a similar explanation for the suicide, that Judas's "soul rushed to Christ on Calvary's mount" to ask and receive forgiveness:[20]

Judas who betrayed and sold the Master after the crucifixion was overwhelmed by a genuine and saving sense of remorse and tried with all his might to draw close to Christ in order to apologize for his betrayal and sale. But since Jesus was accompanied by such a large crowd of people on the way to the mount of Calvary, it was impossible for Judas to come to him and so he said to himself: Since I cannot get to the feet of the master, I will approach him in my spirit at least and humbly ask him for forgiveness. He actually did that and as he took the rope and hanged himself his soul rushed to Christ on Calvary's mount, asked for forgiveness and received it fully from Christ, went up to heaven with him and so his soul enjoys salvation along with all elect.

Yet the all-too-rampant anti-Semitism of the Middle Ages exploited Judas as the arch-betrayer in order to arouse just such sentiments, by painting him as a caricature of a Jew, with exaggerated features, a large hooked nose, red hair, and of course greed for money.

William Klassen has tracked down the sources primarily responsible for the terrible track record of the Dark Ages regarding Judas.[21] First, he lists the *Carmen Paschale* written by Sedulius shortly before 431:

> It is highly likely that Sedulius, more than any other person, is responsible for the negative portrait of Judas so common among the educated, especially the theologians and clergy. "[The *Carmen Paschale*] was required reading in schools throughout the Middle Ages and a source of inspiration for Latin and the vernacular Biblical epics well into the 17th century. . . . It was a work which centuries of European readers found of enduring value," writes a modern student of the epic.

> Sedulius shows no moderation in connection with Judas. His longest literary "intrusion" deals with Judas. His imprecation against Judas, for which there is no biblical precedent, sets the standard for later writers.

The other baleful influence listed by Klassen is the *Legenda Aurea*, the *Golden Legends:*

> The *Legenda Aurea*, a collection of apocryphal stories first gathered by the Dominican Jacob of Virragio (1230–1298), was widely circulated from the fourteenth and fifteenth centuries and beyond. What the *Carmen Paschale* did for the educated, this collection did for the uneducated. It "enveloped the whole intellectual life of the Middle Ages" and, according to one writer, remains the most popular book of edification of the West.

In 1991 Klassen lit upon the sermons of Abraham Santa Clara (actually the Austrian Hans-Ulrich Megerle, 1644–1709), the most eloquent preacher of his day. The title of the work

defaming Judas, when first published (1686–1695), was entitled *Ertz-Schelm*, roughly translated *Prime Slime*. His complete works were published in twenty-one volumes from 1834
to 1954, as well as in a six-volume abbreviated edition (1904–
1907), and his writings have been translated into many languages. Klassen's summary:

> Virtually every Sunday for an entire decade he preached
> about him, or, perhaps better said, *against* him. By way
> of warning to his faithful, Santa Clara proclaimed that
> Judas' mother had talked too much; listeners were urged
> not to let this happen to them lest they bring forth anoth-
> er Judas!
>
> The concluding sermons in his interminable series
> consist of cursing all parts of Judas's anatomy, beginning
> with his red hair and ending with his toes.

Dante Alighieri (1265–1321), in his *Divine Comedy*, relegat-
ed Judas into his Inferno, the lowest (seventh) pit of Hell, where
his head is being gnawed off for all eternity by a three-headed
monster. No doubt he is reunited down there for all eternity
with the other Cainites: Korah, Dathan, and Abiram, "together
with their wives, their children, and their little ones." Those
of you who could not help being a bit sympathetic with these
Cainites, will be appalled by the obvious satisfaction Dante
and others have taken in all this. But those of you who were
even more appalled by the Cainites turning the Bible on its
head, in order to make the bad guys into the good guys, cannot
help but have a bit of sympathy for Dante's presentation. And
this side of the argument has largely prevailed down until relatively modern times.

Part of the blame/credit for this in more recent times goes
to the King James translation of the Bible. King James I of England commissioned a new translation, familiarly known as the

"Authorized Version," which appeared in 1611. It has determined the understanding of the Bible for the English-speaking world ever since. Although the language today sounds quaint, it is perhaps for that very reason still preferred by many who read the Bible. The idea of Judas "betraying" Jesus is deeply imbedded in the King James translation and its successors, and so will be very difficult to eliminate from our cultural tradition. To give you a sense for the language problem, I quote Matthew's treatment of Judas in the King James translation, complete with all its quaintness of "thee-and-thou" language ("ye," "verily," "dippeth," "goeth," "spake," "wherefore," "art")—even its pedantic use of italics for words with no equivalent in the Greek original. I reproduce Matthew, since it has probably been the most widely used by average people over the ages (Matt. 26:14–16, 21–25, 47–50):

14 Then one of the twelve, called Judas Iscariot, went unto the chief priests,

15 And said *unto them*, What will ye give me, and I will deliver him unto you? And they covenanted with him for thirty pieces of silver.

16 And from that time he sought opportunity to betray him. . . .

21 And as they did eat, he said, Verily I say unto you, that one of you shall betray me.

22 And they were exceedingly sorrowful, and began every one of them to say unto him, Lord, is it I?

23 And he answered and said, He that dippeth *his* hand with me in the dish, the same shall betray me.

24 The Son of man goeth as it is written of him: but woe unto that man by whom the Son of man is betrayed! It had been good for that man if he had not been born.

25 Then Judas, which betrayed him, answered and said, Master, is it I? He said unto him, Thou hast said. . . .

47 And while he yet spake, lo, Judas, one of the twelve, came, and with him a great multitude with swords and staves, from the chief priests and elders of the people.

48 Now he that betrayed him gave them a sign, saying, Whomsoever I shall kiss, that same is he: hold him fast.

49 And forthwith he came to Jesus, and said, Hail, master; and kissed him.

50 And Jesus said unto him, Friend, wherefore art thou come? Then came they, and laid hands on Jesus, and took him.

In this imprecise translation, for centuries held as the "gospel truth" by English speakers around the world, Judas comes off as unquestionably dishonorable.

In more recent times, especially since the Enlightenment, views somewhat sympathetic to Judas have emerged. Roger Thiede reports:[22]

Nonetheless the history of the Judas material teaches that the "super-knave," the alleged greedy forefather of all informers and spies, always also found revisionist defenders: Poets such as Klopstock and Goethe, authors such as Walter Jens, belonged here. Also modern theologians, such as the American William Klassen or the German Hans-Josef Klauck, laid out in voluminous monographs the Judas material of the New Testament they interpreted.

Hence "Judas did not betray Christ" is the inference even of the newspaper *Bild*. Basis for the acquittal is especially the significance of the ancient Greek verb *paradidomi*. In most Bible translations the term is translated, in connection with Jesus and Judas, as "betray." To be sure, if one puts the term on the philological gold scales, it is clear that the word in question would be translated as "hand out" or "give over."

Yet the traditional repudiation of Judas continues unabated, as Thiede goes on to point out:

> Yet such subtleties have thus far changed nothing in this, that the name of the perfidious table-companion of Jesus, on the basis of a barely 2000-year-old tradition, is treated by and large as the sum total of the underhandedly disloyal double-dealer.
>
> If an ungrateful football player who is on the rise changes teams behind the back of the team to which he belongs, disillusioned fans still today bawl the name Judas. Also the member of the Kiel assembly, who last week torpedoed the reelection of the SPD Minister President Simonis by his secret abstention, promptly received the biblical reproach.

Yet Thiede also points to a change in attitude in modern times. He captions a picture of Cain killing Abel:[23]

> **Protest against the Good:** The murder of a brother by Cain against Abel has provoked readers of the Bible again and again to risk flirting with evil. Distant influences of Gnosticism showed up also in modern literature.

He then quotes two nineteenth-century romanticists on *The Gospel of Judas*, the German Jewish author Hermann Hesse and the French poet Charles Baudelaire. Following the caption, "Murderers of Brothers and Betrayers," there is the highlighted preview: "Whether there really was the 'Cainite' sect of the church father Irenaeus? In any case it developed literary influence." He points out that Hesse's *Demian* "picked up the theme of Cain":

Using the name "Emil Sinclair" as the author, there appeared in 1919 the novel *Demian*. In reality the author was Hermann Hesse. His book told about a High School student who runs across the theory that one could also conceive of Cain quite differently. "What the story took as its point of departure was the sign. There was a man there who had something in his face that aroused fear in others (. . .) So one explained the sign, not as that which it was, as a distinction, but rather as the opposite. One said that the folk with this sign were weird, and they really were that. People with courage and character are always very weird to the other people. It was very uncomfortable for a race of fearless and weird people to be running around, and so one hung on this race a nickname and a fable, to avenge oneself on it—to hold oneself a bit indemnified for all the fear one endured.

Baudelaire is introduced: "The French lyricist became world famous for his 'Blossoms of Evil'":

> *O, race of Abel, your remains*
> *Rot, wherever the sun burns!*
> *Race of Cain, your works*
> *Are thus not yet at an end;*
> *Race of Abel, in the fray*
> *The lance bored through your flesh!*
> *Race of Cain, go up to heaven,*
> *And hurl God down to earth!*

Will Baudelaire's wish come true, thanks to *The Gospel of Judas*?

In fact, this modern shift in attitude toward Judas is further evidenced by several fictional versions of the long-lost *Gospel of Judas* that have been published over the past century.

The Polish novelist Henryk Panas published *The Gospel of Judas* in 1973.[24] The Irish writer Michael Dickinson wrote *The Lost Testament of Judas Iscariot*, purporting to be Judas's self-defense written to Peter, in 1994.[25] The best was written in 1929 by Ernest Sutherland Bates, *The Gospel of Judas*, portraying Judas as an Essene who continued to reject the God of the Hebrew scriptures that had originally been Jesus's own view.[26] Hugh S. Pyper published in 2001 a very critical survey of such literature, as symptomatic of today's alienation from traditional Christianity and its limitation to the canonical text, now that the Dead Sea Scrolls and the Nag Hammadi Codices have opened up the much broader world of Jewish and Christian texts of the times.[27]

Although it may well strike us as a new and challenging idea, it seems that the attempt to understand Judas's betrayal, to give him the benefit of the doubt and perhaps even redeem him, has a long-standing and continuing tradition.

FOUR

The Gospel of Judas
Surfaces in Geneva

The Gospel of Judas has not been seen for many centuries, having been successfully suppressed by the orthodox church. But the veil of secrecy has just been lifted by Rodolphe Kasser, who announced to the scholarly world the fact that it had surfaced and, incidentally, that he was editing it:[1]

On July 1, 2004, at 11:30 AM the world finally hears more. In the Picard auditorium of a Paris research institute near the Seine, Kasser, the philological Nestor, climbs the platform of the "Eighth International Congress of Coptic Studies," to begin his 20-minute speech, long awaited by the scholarly world, on the topic that, at first glance, seemed harmless, "Un nouvel apocryphe copte" (A New Coptic Apocryphon).

Already after a few sentences it becomes clear that Kasser will celebrate the discovery, as the "extremely seldom and wonderful resurrection" of its main document. It has to do with a work that made a sensation in the second century after Christ, but later again almost completely disappeared from the stage. It really has to do with the copy of the most condemned writing of antiquity: *The Gospel of Judas*, first attested by the church father Irenaeus of Lyon around 180.

Kasser's announcement in Paris on July 1, 2004, of the discovery of *The Gospel of Judas* has produced all-too-sensational German-language articles in journals for the nonscholarly public, first by Ralph Pöhner in the Swiss news magazine *FACTS*,[2] then a cover story by Roger Thiede in its German equivalent *FOCUS*.[3] This was then followed by Robert Macalister Hall's English-language exposé of the Internet attacks by an owner of *The Gospel of Judas*, Mario Jean Roberty, and an antiquities dealer, Michel van Rijn.[4] Both Pöhner and Hall interviewed me by phone from Zürich and London while preparing their articles, without my answers to their questions seeming to have much effect on what they wrote. The result is that these journalistic essays, which apparently first opened up the story to a wider public, function as a very entertaining, if not very enlightening, by-product of the otherwise sensational-enough story of *The Gospel of Judas*.

The essay by Pöhner, entitled "Judas the Hero," begins, just below the title, with the summary:

> It is almost as old as the gospels of salvation of the New Testament—and shows a completely other view of the betrayer of Jesus. For centuries the "Gospel of Judas" was missing. Now the early Christian writing reappears. It is in Switzerland.

Pöhner quite rightly quotes scholars in the field to underline the importance of *The Gospel of Judas:* Ludwig Koenen, professor of classics at the University of Michigan, reported that "there was no doubt as to its authenticity"; "in my capacity I could judge that." Steve Emmel, professor of Coptic studies at the University of Münster, Germany: "of extraordinary interest." Peter Nagel, professor of church history at the University of Bonn, Germany: "very, very valuable." And Charles Hedrick, professor of religious studies emeritus at Missouri State University: "It is always exciting when one discovers a lost Gospel. This one here will help us to complete the scintillating picture of Christianity in the second century."

Indeed, scholars assume that *The Gospel of Judas* was written somewhat more than a century after Jesus's death. As we have seen, the standard edition of the apocryphal New Testament books states:

> Dating: *The Gospel of Judas* was of course composed before 180, the date at which it is mentioned for the first time by Irenaeus in *adv. Haer.* If it is in fact a Cainite work, and if this sect—assuming it was an independent Gnostic group—was constituted in part, as has sometimes been asserted, in dependence on the doctrine of Marcion, the apocryphon can scarcely have been composed before the middle of the 2nd century. This would, however, be to build on weak arguments. At most we may be inclined to suspect a date between 130 and 170 or thereabouts.

But *The Gospel of Judas* disappeared soon afterward, and wasn't seen again until 1983. The University of Michigan is the American university with the strongest tradition of acquiring and editing papyrus manuscripts. And in 1975, Michigan reinforced this reputation by luring from the German University of Cologne to its Classics Department, a distinguished expert with quite a track record of his own for acquiring and editing papyrus manuscripts, Ludwig Koenen. Perhaps he is best known for the Cologne Mani Codex, a miniature biography of the third-century Persian founder of the dualistic religion of Manichaeism, which is today the star exhibit in the papyrus collection of the University of Cologne. It is so miniature that it can hardly be read with the naked eye, and must have served more as an amulet to bring good luck than as a book to put on the shelf, much less to read.

Since Koenen had good connections both inside and outside Egypt for acquiring manuscripts, it is no coincidence that it is he who was invited to come to Geneva to meet with a Copt from Egypt and a Greek from Athens who had important manuscripts for sale. Koenen had received a few photographs of very bad quality, presumably so that they could not be used for unauthorized publication, but good enough to indicate the importance of the papyrus manuscripts. He had been able to identify one as a Greek mathematical text, in which he was primarily interested, and another as the book of Exodus in Greek, in which his Old Testament colleague David Noel Friedman was interested. So the two of them resolved to fly to Geneva and negotiate the purchase. But a third was written in Coptic, which neither of them could read, and which neither was interested in purchasing.

Koenen knew that I was working in Coptic, as the American representative on the International Committee for the Nag Hammadi Codices. Hence Koenen approached me as to whether I would be interested in participating in the negotiations (and funding), so as to acquire the manuscripts in Geneva. He was flying to Geneva in May 1983 to meet with the sellers, and hoped to consummate a deal for their purchase while there.

I was not free to go to Geneva on a moment's notice, and the Institute for Antiquity and Christianity of which I was director did not have funds for such an acquisition, no matter how tempting it might be. But I did the best I could under the circumstances. I had brought together a team of young American scholars to edit the Nag Hammadi Codices, and so I sent out an urgent appeal to them to see what they could do to make this venture possible.

The only member of our team who was able to offer any assistance was Harold W. Attridge of Southern Methodist University. Harry had been a Junior Fellow at Harvard, the highest distinction a graduate student there could receive. Then Harry moved to his first teaching position at the Perkins School of Theology at Southern Methodist University in Dallas, Texas. Harry later moved on to Notre Dame, where he became dean, and from there to Yale University, where he is currently dean of the Divinity School.

Harry secured a pledge from the acquisitions funds of the Bridwell Library at Perkins School of Theology, authorized by Deckerd Turner, the divinity librarian at the time, for the total budget for the year, $50,000. Harry reports that "Mr. Turner and Bridwell had a fund for the purchase of rare and theologically significant books and he was happy to collaborate with the effort to acquire the codices." Harry notified me promptly that this money could be made available for the Geneva venture.[5] It is interesting that the manuscripts would actually be seen by Attridge years later when he was at Yale.

Since I did not have sufficient funds to make the trip from California to Geneva to verify the value of the Coptic manuscript and negotiate its purchase, I thought the best I could do was to fund the trip for a former student of mine, Stephen Emmel, who was doing research at the time with Tito Orlandi, Italy's foremost Coptic scholar, in Rome, which was a less expensive "short" train trip from Geneva. I persuaded Steve to go to Geneva on my behalf.

Steve had become fascinated with Gnosticism when he was still in college and part of the student culture that grew out of resistance to the Vietnam War. Like most college students of the time, he knew all about taking trips through the heavens, but he determined that "thinking is the best way to travel." He came across Gnosticism in an introductory course on Judaism and Christianity in 1970 and then happened to get hold of Hans Jonas's *The Gnostic Religion*,[6] a book that made existential sense for him of the complicated mythology of Gnosticism, with its message of Gnostics escaping this evil world below by flying through the skies to the higher unknown God above. Nothing would do but that Steve had to learn about these ancient "hippies," whose secrets were due to be revealed in the still unpublished Nag Hammadi Codices. Steve recalls,

> I became interested in Coptic history while I was a student at Syracuse University in the United States at the beginning of the 1970s. I was interested in philosophy and religion—all the philosophies and religions—as different ways in which human beings have searched for truth and the meaning of life. In an introductory university course about Judaism and Christianity, I discovered the ancient Gnosis or Gnosticism, and I learnt that most of the original ancient Gnostic sources were written in Coptic. The most important sources are the Nag Hammadi codices, which are ancient papyrus books written in Coptic. I was so interested in reading these books that I learnt Coptic, and came to Cairo in 1974 to work on them at the Coptic Museum with my university professor, James M. Robinson.

Steve found out that I was the person in America at the center of efforts to break the monopoly so as to get access to these new manuscripts, and so he came to study with me. That was just when I was about to go to Cairo for a sabbatical in order to reassemble the fragmentary leaves of the codices so that they could be photographed and published, the way I had figured out to break the monopoly. He tagged along . . . and ended up the best conservator of papyrus anywhere! Steve stayed on in Cairo long after my sabbatical was over, to complete the work of assembling the fragments to restore the leaves.[7] And so he was still in Cairo at the right time to help me, from a distance, organize the First International Congress of Coptology and found the International Association for Coptic Studies.

Steve has advanced brilliantly throughout his career, ending up in the only permanent Chair of Coptic Studies in the world, at the University of Münster, Germany. The Institute for Egyptology and Coptology, where he works there, is in effect the Secretariat of the International Association for Coptic Studies he helped me found. He edits its *Newsletter* and helps to organize its congresses every four years. Indeed, he was closely involved in organizing the most recent congress in Paris, in 2004, where *The Gospel of Judas* was first announced.

Koenen and Friedman took the plane from Ann Arbor, and Steve took the train from Rome. On May 15, 1983, they met in Geneva in a hotel room with a Copt from Egypt, who spoke no English, and a Greek from Athens, John Perdios, who spoke English and functioned as translator.

Perdios had grown up in the international society of Cairo. But with the Egyptian revolution that deposed King Farouk and created a socialist state, most of the well-to-do foreign colony left. Though Perdios now lived in Athens, he stayed in contact with his Coptic friend, for they had been classmates in Cairo. Obviously Perdios was functioning as the intermediary for the Coptic owner in the transaction.

Steve has recently described what went on:[8]

That was in 1983. At the time I did not know that it had to do with *The Gospel of Judas*. The codex contained three writings. I could identify on the spot the second text. I could also see the third part, a dialogue between Jesus and the disciples. I even read the name Judas. Only I did not see the line "The Gospel of Judas."

When asked why he did not see the title, he replied:

The circumstances under which we had to work were very unfavorable. The examination took place in a hotel.

We only had half an hour time, and were not permitted to take any photographs, or write anything. The papyrus leaves were very fragile. So I could peep in only here and there.

Malcolm Macalister Hall, another journalist reporting on the story, quoted Steve in considerably more detail:[9]

"We were given about half an hour to look into what were effectively three shoeboxes, with the papyri wrapped up in newspapers," says Emmel. "We weren't allowed to make any photographs, or take any notes. The people who had them knew really nothing about them except that they were valuable—and that they wanted money."

The bundles included a mathematical treatise, and the Book of Exodus, both in Greek. Emmel saw that the Coptic manuscripts—in a single leather-bound volume with its back cover missing—included *The First Apocalypse of James* and *The Letter of Peter to Philip* (both already known to scholars from a huge collection of ancient manuscripts which had been found in the 1940s, known as the Nag Hammadi Library). But there was another manuscript too. It appeared to be a dialogue between Jesus and his disciples. Emmel saw the name Judas, but, because the papyrus was in such fragile condition and beginning to crumble, he could only lift each page slightly with his philatelist's tweezers, and could not see any title page. However, he deduced—correctly, as it turned out—that this was a previously unknown work of Gnostic literature, and unique. (An early sect within Christianity, the Gnostics were repeatedly denounced as heretics.)

To Emmel, the meeting had an air of cloak-and-dagger, and he suspected that the papyri had been smuggled. "The indication was that these were people who were not exactly working in bright daylight," he says. "I think there was no question but that this material should have still been in Egypt." And the price came as a shock.

"They were asking $3m—and they said that this was down from the original asking price of $10m. I don't know if that was true—I think this was just a way of saying $3m was a bargain. They were not interested in selling any of the items separately. And my budget from Southern Methodist was just $50,000. We were flabbergasted by this price."

Emmel says Professor Ludwig Koenen—the leader of the academic party—then went into the bathroom with the Egyptian, to negotiate. "When they came out I could see on Koenen's face it was a no-go," Emmel recalls. Banned from taking notes, he had all the while been desperately trying to commit to memory all the details of the texts he had seen. When the two sides then had a valedictory lunch together after the failed deal, Emmel made his excuses, slipped out to the lavatory, pulled a scrap of paper from his pocket and noted down everything he could recall. He never saw the manuscript again. . . .

Stephen Emmel agrees that this has been just another disaster for Coptology. "It is, but we're used to it," he says, resignedly. "Coptic manuscripts in general have not survived well. It's not anything new, but it's sad because if scientists could have taken that manuscript out of its shoebox in that hotel-room in Geneva in 1983 and worked on it, we would have had a very well-preserved manuscript. Now we've got another collection of fragments. We may never be able to restore it fully."

A Dutch reporter, Henk Schutten, also quoted Steve in some detail:[10]

The meeting was extremely secretive, the manuscripts were smuggled out of Egypt, so much was clear. Questions about the origin were not appreciated.

They were not experts. They believed that there were three manuscripts, but there were actually four. After a quick listing, we learned that they dated from about the fourth or the fifth century AD. Two manuscripts, a translation of the Book of Exodus and a mathematical essay, were written in Greek. They were packed in separate boxes just like some letters of Paul the Disciple also written in Coptic (old Egyptian).

They were held together by a leather strap and the edges should have been intact back then. Its owners have not cared much for the find. Only half of the strap and part of the probable cover had been preserved and there were holes and tears in the pages.

The numbers of the pages went up to sixty, while most papyrus-codices are at least twice as big. I suspected half of the manuscript to be missing.

When asked what he thought when he saw the name Judas, Steve replied:[11]

The name was not decisive. Just as any knowledgeable person would have done, I assumed that it had to do with the namesake of Judas Iscariot, the disciple Judas Didymos Thomas. He occurs often in apocryphal Gospels, more often than Judas Iscariot. It is also for him that *The Gospel of Thomas* is named. If I had seen the title at the end, it would of course have immediately occurred to me that Iscariot was meant, especially since right above it, as the last sentence of the text, there stands: "Judas took some money and handed him over."

The sale price was $3,000,000, which of course was far more than the potential purchasers could produce. Perdios later reported to me that Friedman had said off-handedly that the owner should drop one zero from the asking price. Of course, when bargaining in the bazaar, it is expected that one will not pay the first asking price, but will negotiate down to a mutually agreeable price. This is the world in which the owner had always lived and understood quite well. But it would be considered an insult for the first counteroffer to be only 10 percent of the asking price, as if the seller knows nothing of the value of his wares or is simply trying to milk the potential buyer. Hence, the owner was offended. The negotiations ended before they had really begun. In any case, they would hardly have succeeded, since a tenth of the three million was probably as much or more than the purchasers would have been able to produce. In fact, Steve is reported to have said:[12] "We could perhaps have paid a tenth." The three codices were not acquired, and the three potential purchasers went away empty-handed.

Almost! Steve had been less involved in the negotiations themselves, and had been able to focus instead on the Coptic codex. He was permitted to examine the Coptic leaves in enough detail to be able to decide, primarily on the basis of their dimensions, that they were really all that was left of *two* Coptic codices. This was kept secret from the sellers, since it looked as if they had set the asking price at the round figure of a million dollars per codex. Obviously the potential purchasers did not want the price to jump to $4,000,000!

After the negotiations had failed, they nonetheless all went out for lunch together, which was when Steve excused himself to go to the bathroom and transcribe what his acute eye had seen and memory had retained of the Coptic material. He afterward wrote his notes in a confidential memorandum, which he sent to me. We did not want it made public at the time, lest it get back to the sellers and escalate still further the asking price. But its details can now be made public, since the purchase has been consummated (at an unknown price, but surely much less than was asked for in Geneva). As a result, nothing is to be gained by further confidentiality. His report is hence published for the first time at the conclusion of this chapter.

Steve identified three Coptic tractates, two of which are familiar from duplicates in the Nag Hammadi Codices: one was a copy of *The First Apocalypse of James* known from Nag Hammadi Codex V, Tractate 4,[13] and one a copy of *The Letter of Peter to Philip* known from Nag Hammadi Codex VIII, Tractate 2. There was no way to know whether there were more than three tractates. Of course Steve could not sort through the whole stack of fragile papyrus leaves with his "philatelist's tweezers," but had to "peep in only here and there." This comment is an important detail, since it indicates that journalists' statements referring to the number of leaves in the lot purchased by the Maecenas Foundation are no more than speculation. Only when the leaves are assembled from fragments and conserved between panes of glass can one speak about how many leaves, in whole or part, have been rescued.

Steve could only identify the third tractate, a previously unknown text, as a dialogue between Jesus and his disciples (a standard Gnostic literary genre), though he happened to observe the name Judas. This is what is now known as *The Gospel of Judas*. But he did not identify the Judas in question as Judas Iscariot. As he explained in the interview quoted above, the normal assumption would be that "Judas" referred to Didymos Judas Thomas, since he is listed as the author of two Nag Hammadi tractates (II, 2 and 7). Codex II, Tractate 2, is *The Gospel of Thomas*. It begins:

These are the hidden words that the living Jesus spoke. And Didymos Judas Thomas wrote them down.

This introduction seems to have been echoed at the beginning of Nag Hammadi Codex II, Tractate 7, *The Book of Thomas.*

> The hidden words that the savior spoke to Judas Thomas which I, even I, Mathaias, wrote down, while I was walking, listening to them speak with one another. The savior said, "Brother Thomas, while you have time in the world, listen to me, and I will reveal to you the things you have pondered in your mind. Now since it has been said that you are my twin and true companion, examine yourself and learn who you are, in which way you exist, and how you will come to be."

All this is clearly a play on the name Didymos Judas Thomas with which *The Gospel of Thomas* begins. *Didymos* is the Greek word for "twin," and *Thomas* is the Semitic word for "twin." So both of these Nag Hammadi tractates are ascribed to a person named Judas and nicknamed "Twin."

In the Gospel of John (11:16; 20:24; 21:2), this Judas is simply named Thomas, with the added translation, "called the Twin," here using the Greek word *Didymos.* He is considered one of the inner circle, but is not identified as Jesus's brother. Nor is the nickname Twin explained. He is most familiar to us as the "doubting Thomas," due to his insistence that he touch Jesus's wounds before he will believe that it is the same person who was crucified (John 20:25, 27–28). So it would be logical for Steve to assume this tractate was ascribed to the disciple Judas known as "Doubting Thomas," rather than to Judas Iscariot, the disciple who betrayed Jesus.

The very fact that two of the three tractates that are in the codex containing *The Gospel of Judas* are duplicates of Nag Hammadi tractates has misled some into thinking that this new codex, discovered no doubt shortly before being shown in

Geneva in 1983, is part of the Nag Hammadi discovery of 1945. But this is not the case, for a number of reasons.

It would be a misunderstanding of the collection of codices that were discovered near Nag Hammadi. When one examines distinguishing characteristics, such as the technique in manufacturing the leather covers, the different scribal hands involved in copying the codices, and the differences in Coptic dialect among the translations of tractates, one notes that they tend to fall into four clusters. But there are no duplicates within a single cluster, only in different clusters. Hence if the codex with *The Gospel of Judas* had been part of the Nag Hammadi discovery, one would have to rule that this one codex was a fifth separate cluster of tractates, only secondarily brought together with the Nag Hammadi Codices.

There is already an instance of duplicates with Nag Hammadi tractates in a codex that we know was not part of the Nag Hammadi discovery: a century ago a codex was discovered and deposited in Berlin, named Papyrus Berolinensis 8502, which has duplicates of two Nag Hammadi tractates, as well as two tractates not found in Nag Hammadi, the most famous of which is *The Gospel of Mary*.[14] So the existence of duplicate tractates does not mean that both copies came from the same discovery.

What the public does not realize is that Coptic manuscript discoveries are taking place in Egypt on an almost regular basis since the Nag Hammadi discovery, and no one has suggested that these come from Nag Hammadi.[15] The fact that the discovery that included *The Gospel of Judas* also involved a Greek mathematical text and a Greek copy of the Psalms, as well as a Coptic copy of Pauline Epistles, does not suggest that these materials were part of the Nag Hammadi discovery.

Yet the idea that *The Gospel of Judas* was part of the Nag Hammadi discovery seems not to want to go away, so let me try to put it to rest once and for all:

Stephen C. Carlson reports:[16]

Roger Pearse of the Tertullian Project had put together a history of the discovery of the Nag Hammadi Library ("The Nag Hammadi discovery of manuscripts," July 30, 2003). Of possible relevance to *The Gospel of Judas* is this bit of information (**emphasis** added):

The books were divided among the 7 camel-drivers present. According to 'Ali there were 13 (our 'codex XIII' was not included in the number, as it was inside codex VI). **Thus a codex was lost more or less at the site.** Seven lots were drawn up. Covers were removed and each consisted of a complete codex plus part of another. The other drivers, ignorant of the value and afraid of sorcery and Muhammad 'Ali, disclaimed any share, whereon he piled them all back together.

This presentation, which is used by Carlson to suggest (**boldface**) that there is a missing Nag Hammadi codex, is an oversimplified summary of a report I made in 1979, which actually pointed in the opposite direction. So I need to quote my own presentation to straighten things out:[17]

Muhammad 'Ali decided to divide the codices on the spot among the seven camel drivers present. Evidence of only 12 codices survives today. What is called Codex XIII consists of only eight leaves, which were removed from the center of the codex in late antiquity in order to separate out a tractate inscribed on them and then laid inside the front cover of Codex VI. These leaves probably would not even have been noticed by the discoverers, much less considered a separate codex. Yet when pressed, Muhammad 'Ali maintained that the number of codices in the jar was not 12 but 13. Thus it is possible, though unconfirmed, that a quite fragmentary codex was completely lost at the cliff. Since the number of codices was fewer than enough for each camel driver to receive 2, Muhammad 'Ali prepared seven lots each consisting of a complete codex and parts of the others torn up for this purpose. Muhammad 'Ali has maintained that covers were abandoned at the cliff, which would account for the missing cover of Codex XII as well as for that of any unattested cover. The other camel drivers, ignorant of the value inherent in the codices and fearing both sorcery and Muhammad 'Ali, renounced their claims to a share. He then stacked the lots back together in a pile, unwound his white headdress, knotted them in it, and slung the whole bundle over his shoulder. Unhobbling his camel, he rode back to his home in al-Qasr, in the courtyard of which the animals were kept and bread baked in the large clay oven. Here he dumped the codices, loose leaves and fragments, on the ground among the straw that was lying by the oven to be burned. 'Umm Ahmad [his mother] has conceded that she burned much of the ripped-out papyrus and broken covers, perhaps parts of the covers of XI and XII, in the oven along with the straw.

The removal of leaves from their cover at the cliff and the subsequent burning of some in the oven may be correlated to some extent with the condition in which the material was first examined and recorded in detail. If another codex existed, no trace of it has been brought to light, since the surviving unplaced fragments either seem to have the same scribal hands as do the codices that survive, and hence, presumably, to have come from them, or are too small or preserve too little ink to provide a basis for conjecturing the existence of further codices.

Muhammad 'Ali had heard me and others talk of thirteen codices, and so he would quite naturally speak of thirteen, not recalling what he had counted at the time (if he had counted at all—he was illiterate). In all probability he was just playing back what he had learned was the "correct" number. In any case, his report of what happened at the time of the discovery would not indicate that a previously unknown codex containing *The Gospel of Judas* survived to appear a generation later. Rather his report would indicate that anything that has not reached its final destination in the Coptic Museum in Cairo was shredded at the cliff or burned in his mother's oven. There is no way that his report can be twisted into the suggestion that *The Gospel of Judas* was in a codex from the Nag Hammadi discovery. Yet it goes on.

Henk Schutten interviewed the most famous Dutch Nag Hammadi expert, and reported:[18]

> [Gilles] Quispel does not exclude that the Gospel of Judas has the same origin as the Nag Hammadi documents.

Quispel was the Dutch representative on the International Committee for the Nag Hammadi Codices of which I was permanent secretary, and it is he who went to Belgium to take possession of Nag Hammadi Codex I on behalf of the Jung Institute of Zürich. But I have been through his archives, which he entrusted to me for preservation in the Nag Hammadi Archives I have collected, and Quispel has no information on this topic. There is nothing in them that would indicate any connection of *The Gospel of Judas* with the Nag Hammadi Codices.

Yet Schutten reports Quispel as saying:

> "[J]udging by its content, it is clearly a Gnostic document. There is a reference to Allogenes, also called Seth, the third son of Adam and Eve. In Jewish gnosis Seth is viewed as the Saviour." In many old documents from the first years of Christianity references to *The Gospel of Judas*

can be found, says Quispel. But after being banned by the Church, the manuscript seemed to have disappeared from the face of the earth. Not surprising, according to Quispel: "Gnosis is the most persecuted religion in the world. Followers were put to death by the Catholic Church. He who possessed the manuscript risked his life." Religious historians assume that the Gospel of Judas has been written in the same period as the canonical gospels of Mark, Matthew, Luke and John. Because the Judas-manuscript is written in Coptic—the last stage of Old-Egyptian—it is assumed that this is a copy translated from Greek from the original text presumably from the first or second century. Is the Gospel written by Judas? That is a difficult question to answer for Quispel. "I doubt it very much, but you can never entirely exclude this option." An obvious conclusion is that this text is from an Early-Christian Sect, called the Kainite. . . .

Till middle of last century what was known about old Gnostics was mainly based on documents of the Catholic Church that fought the doctrine with fire and brimstone. This changed when in 1945 farmers found an urn in Nag Hammadi in Upper-Egypt containing 12 books— or codices, written on papyrus and held together with a leather strap. The Nag Hammadi Codices consist of 52 documents, most of them with Gnostic intent. The most famous document out [of] this collection, *The Gospel of Thomas*, was purchased by Professor Quist [Van Rijn's play on the name Quispel] in 1952.

Just like the Gospel of Judas, the Nag Hammadi–documents ended up in the hands of money hungry art dealers, among them a Belgian dealer. . . . Quispel wrote to several sponsors when he heard of the discovery. With a cheque for 35,000 Swiss Francs in his pocket he finally got

on the train to Brussels on May 10th, 1952. "A mere tri-
fle, even in those days, but I did return to the Netherlands
with the manuscript. Nowadays, these documents would
be worth four to five million dollars." Quispel does not
exclude that the Gospel of Judas has the same origin as the
Nag Hammadi–documents. He remembers how in 1955 he
visited Tano, a Cypriot dealer in Cairo with a large number
of documents, upon request of Queen Juliana who showed
a lot of interest in the Gnostics. "The Egyptian authorities
seized Tano's collection, but he wrote to me later on that
he left for Geneva to offer some documents for sale that
he was able to smuggle out of Egypt to Martin Bodmer, a
rich Swiss. It would not surprise Quispel that the Gospel
of Judas fell into the hands of Bodmer through the same
Phokion Tano.

"Bodmer placed the documents in a Swiss foundation
named after him. He hired a Swiss minister who taught
himself Coptic to translate it. This minister, Rodolphe
Kasser, is the man who is finalizing the translation of the
Gospel of Judas."

For Quispel to suggest that Tano sold it to Bodmer is utterly ridiculous. It may have found its way recently into the Bibliothèque
Bodmer near Geneva to be conserved and studied, after having
been offered for sale in Geneva a generation earlier (1983), and
after having wandered to New York, Yale University, and elsewhere. But all of those travels would not have taken place if Tano
had sold it to Bodmer! He would have promptly deposited it in
the Bibliothèque Bodmer, just as he did his other acquisitions.

Quispel's pupil and successor, as the much more distinguished Dutch authority on Gnosticism, is Hans van Oort. His
more sober news release is also translated by Michel Van Rijn,
with the title: "Gospel of Judas not by Judas":[19]

The owner of the text, who only wants to make money from it, has carefully timed the publicity surrounding what is called *The Gospel of Judas*. That is the opinion of Prof. Hans van Oort, who specializes in Gnosticism, Manichaeism, Nag Hammadi and Augustine. He called a press conference on his own initiative, to counter "all the nonsense" being written at the moment about *The Gospel of Judas;* for example that the Vatican has an interest in the document's not being published. . . .

Van Oort does not rule out that it involves the missing codex from the Nag Hammadi codices. What he does rule out is that Judas himself wrote it: "There is no reason whatsoever to assume that he did this. Nothing points to that.". . .

Van Oort is one of the few people who knows the contents of *The Gospel of Judas,* but does not want any trouble with its owner, the Swiss Maecenas Foundation. "If I did, I would be killed."

Yet I had first mentioned the discovery of the codex containing *The Gospel of Judas* in print precisely in order to make clear that it was not part of the Nag Hammadi discovery:[20]

There have emerged no cogent reasons to postulate that there were more [than thirteen Nag Hammadi codices]. For though a sizable part of a Fourth Century Gnostic codex was seen by Ludwig Koenen and Stephen Emmel in Europe in 1983, containing a different version of *The (First) Apocalypse of James* and a copy of *The Letter of Peter to Philip* (with this as its subscript title), as well as a previously unknown dialogue between Jesus and his disciples, it is associated provisionally with a different provenience than Nag Hammadi and should not, without some positive evidence to that effect, e.g. from physical traits or from the cartonnage, be identified as a Nag Hammadi codex.

By "physical traits" I had in mind the handwriting, the technique in manufacturing the quire(s) and the leather cover. And by "the cartonnage" I had in mind references to places and names often found in the trash papyrus used to thicken and line the cover. No such supporting evidence has emerged. There is absolutely no reason to assume that the manuscript containing *The Gospel of Judas* was part of the Nag Hammadi discovery. The place where it is reported to have been discovered is much farther down the Nile, nearer where the Oxyrhynchus manuscripts (an enormous horde of ancient texts including many New Testament papyri) were discovered a century ago. And yet the association with Nag Hammadi is too good to let go of easily. Michel van Rijn comments, without any information to go on:[21]

> The manuscript was dug up at near Nag Hammadi, then illegally exported from Egypt and illegally imported in the US, where Frieda acquired it.

At first I had hesitated to publish anything about the discovery of this previously unknown Coptic manuscript, lest it get back somehow to the owner or his agent, and they raise their asking price accordingly. But Steve's report did have scholarly information that colleagues would of course be eager to know. I was particularly pleased that Steve had been able to read the title of the second tractate, *The Letter of Peter to Philip*. The copy in Nag Hammadi Codex VIII, Tractate 2, has a title set off at its beginning that reads more fully: *The Letter of Peter Which He Sent to Philip*. But I had, for purely practical reasons, abbreviated it, for use by scholars, to precisely the title that turned up on the new copy: "The Letter of Peter to Philip."

I passed on the information at the time to Hans-Gebhard Bethge, since he was writing a dissertation (at Humboldt University, Berlin, 1984) on *The Letter of Peter to Philip*, and he mentioned in print this second copy:[22]

> Ep. Pet. Phil. however was also handed down outside the Nag Hammadi codices, but the text of the parallel version is so far not yet available for scholarly evaluation.

In a footnote he explained how he had heard about it:

> The first information about the existence of this text, which is in a papyrus codex along with a version of 1 Apoc. Jas. and a dialogue of Jesus with his disciples not identical with NCH III 5, was given by J. M. Robinson and S. Emmel at the Third International Congress of Coptic Studies in Warsaw in August 1984.

At that time in Warsaw, we would never have dreamed that it would take twenty years, until the *Eighth* International Congress of Coptic Studies, in Paris, before we would learn on July 1, 2004, what the dialogue of Jesus with his disciples was: *The Gospel of Judas!*

My student Marvin W. Meyer, who was preparing the critical edition of *The Letter of Peter to Philip*, also included in it a reference to the duplicate copy in 1991:[23]

> According to the reports of James M. Robinson and Stephen Emmel, a somewhat divergent Coptic text of *The Letter of Peter to Philip* is to be found in a papyrus codex which at the present time is neither published nor available for study.

I had forwarded to Meyer in March 1991 what I could read from the blurred photographs that I had received from Koenen. He published this very fragmentary transcription, parallel to the text of Nag Hammadi Codex VIII, 135,25–136,2. (Marv, like Harry Attridge and Steve Emmel, will reemerge a generation later as a major player in the story.)

It is striking that Rodolphe Kasser, when he announced on July 1, 2004, in Paris that he had been authorized to publish the manuscript of *The Gospel of Judas*, made no reference to these previously published bits of information about the codex. It is normally the scholarly way of doing things, to begin with references to previous publications about such a new text. Surely he knew about them, for he was the Swiss representative on the International Committee for the Nag Hammadi Codices. Prior to the publication of each volume in *The Facsimile Edition of the Nag Hammadi Codices*, which was theoretically authorized and supervised by that Committee, I sent each member a prepublication copy for review, and they all received complimentary copies of each volume as it was published, from the publisher, E. J. Brill. Furthermore, the places where Bethge and Meyer published their comments were the kinds of publications that, though too esoteric for the sellers to know about, were precisely the kinds of standard scholarly tools that were of course on Kasser's bookshelf. Kasser's presentation in Paris of a new manuscript discovery seemed more sensational by omitting any reference to it having already been mentioned in publications years ago. What was in fact the only new thing in Kasser's sensational speech was the title of the last tractate in the manuscript, *The Gospel of Judas*.

The experience of not being able to engender enough funds to negotiate successfully for the purchase of the manuscripts in 1983 made me realize that having contacts with wealthy patrons collecting such things might prove useful, if ever I hoped to reopen these negotiations. So I was able to interest

Martin Schøyen, a wealthy Norwegian collector of ancient manuscripts, in acquiring them.

In the late 1980s I was frequently passing through Athens, usually on my way to Egypt to work on the Nag Hammadi Codices. So I made a serious effort to track down the Athenian person whom Steve had met in Geneva. Naturally, I inquired of Koenen, for he had no doubt set up the Geneva meeting through this Athenian as the intermediary, with whom he may well have had previous experience in acquiring manuscripts for the collection at Cologne. Koenen was kind enough to give me his name, John Perdios, and his phone number in Athens, at a travel agency operated by his brother.

I went to Athens, and he received me in his elegant home. His own specialty was buying and selling paintings of the nineteenth century Bavarian tradition because, he explained, Greece had imported a royal family from Bavaria at the time, and imported along with the royal family their Bavarian art and paintings. Perdios took me to dinner at the best outdoor restaurant in Athens, to go over, in such a leisurely atmosphere, plans for acquiring the manuscripts. The outcome was that he agreed to meet Schøyen and me in New York along with the Coptic owner.

Perdios never divulged to me the full name of the owner, perhaps lest he be charged by the Egyptian government with illegal excavation and exportation, and/or lest Perdios be bypassed in favor of direct negotiations with the Coptic owner. Perdios would of course not want to be cut out of his share of the profit! He did give the person's name as Hannah, but this, a nickname for Greek and Coptic Johannes, English John, would not serve to identify him for me or for the Egyptian authorities, since it is as common a name among Copts as it is among Christians elsewhere. ("John" Perdios is of course just the anglicized form of his Greek name, Johannes.)

I inquired why he proposed New York for the meeting. He said his brother lived there, and he would like to visit him. I assumed that the more basic reason was that the codices were there. He would have known that we would want to see them before committing ourselves, and indeed would want to take possession of them if the negotiations succeeded. Of course I could only conjecture that they might be in the custody of his brother, or of someone in the large Coptic community of New Jersey. They are now reported to have been in a safety deposit box in Citibank, Hicksville, Long Island, New York. Michel van Rijn has been even more specific:[24]

> After Hannah and Koutoulakis worked out their differences, the gospel was sent to a cousin of Hannah in NY, without declaring it at customs.

Schøyen agreed to attend the meeting on a date in January 1991 agreeable to the sellers. I had gone so far as to check out New York hotels! Thus, we were actively making preparations late in 1990 for the meeting. But just at this time Iraqi president Saddam Hussein decided he needed to annex Kuwait to expand his oil empire on the way to Saudi Arabia. President George H. W. Bush sent him an ultimatum to withdraw, with the threat that if he did not do so the United States would begin bombing Baghdad in January. Thereupon I received word from Perdios that the Copt was not willing to abandon his family at the beginning of World War III. The trip had to be called off!

Early in 1992 I was a guest professor at the University of Geneva, and phoned Perdios from there, in case I needed to go quickly to Athens to see about setting up the New York meeting again. He said he would contact his Coptic friend, when the friend next came from Middle Egypt to Cairo, and would let me know. But I never heard from him again. The meeting never took place. But my interest in these elusive Coptic codices did not die.

A French Canadian team of scholars at Laval University in Québec is publishing the French edition of the Nag Hammadi Codices, and I have functioned as a consultant for the Canada Council on their behalf. They have also received grants from the Canadian Bombardier Foundation. They thought that this foundation might also fund the acquisition of the new Coptic manuscripts that Steve Emmel had viewed in Geneva, making it possible for them to stay together as a team and continue their work even after the completion of their edition of the Nag Hammadi Codices.

Their funding from the Canada Council included a stipend for a visiting professor in Coptic, to strengthen their own limited faculty resources. They had once inquired of me if I could recommend someone. I suggested one of the world's leading Coptic scholars, the German Wolf-Peter Funk, whom I expected to see shortly when I visited East Berlin. As it turned out, I was approaching Funk at a propitious time, and he expressed his willingness to go to Canada, where he has been ever since as the authority on Coptic grammar in charge of Laval's ongoing seminar as they prepare each volume for publication. But he has no permanent chair at the university, so that his future, after the completion of the Nag Hammadi project, is uncertain. It is understandable that the Laval team hoped that they could acquire the new Coptic manuscripts. I told them how they could contact Perdios by phone, and a member of their team, the Norwegian Einar Thomassen, did phone him in September 2001, but nothing came of it. Of course by this time the manuscripts had long since been sold. Thus my efforts to acquire the new Gnostic manuscripts came to naught.

Despite his opening claim to the contrary, a sensationalistic, and perhaps to some extent fictional, version of the selling of *The Gospel of Judas* was published in a German news magazine by Roger Thiede:[25]

The following story is true, even though on first glance it might seem to be a remake of John Huston's film "The Maltese Falcon."

His story begins:[26]

At the endless haggling over the coveted antiquity in the Swiss hotel room, there surface first of all: the unscrupulous jeweler Hannah from Cairo, who wants to hawk an anthology with three early Christian tractates in a foreign country, in a very stubborn way for exactly three million dollars, no cent less; further, as buyer, the art dealer who was a resident of Geneva, Nikolas Koutoulakis.

He then provides otherwise unattested information about the provenience:[27]

The mysterious manuscript had survived 1600 years in a stone box in the desert sand of the Middle-Egyptian location Muh Zafat al-Minya.

Then the story promptly turns sexy:[28]

Now, to be sure, its last hour threatens. For the pair of dealers have a falling out with each other. The cause is the indispensable *femme fatale*, who, as fits her genre, sees to it that there is chaos. Due to his lack of knowledge of human nature, Koutoulakis wants to entrust to his young love Mia detailed negotiations—promptly the lady attempts to get one over on him. In the counter-attack the furious sugar daddy forces his way into the apartment of the Egyptian. In the tumult the loot is ripped crosswise. Large parts land in Mia's purse, and then evaporate for a long time. One folio leaf is lost forever. The remainder Koutoulakis is able to secure. Later the Greek avenges himself on the Cairo opponent: Massive threats of murder had their effect.

Michel Van Rijn tells the story on his Web site briefly, though with more detail, not to say humor:[29]

Egyptian jeweller Hannah received a stone box from a man who thought he'd come across something big. What he found was unbelievably huge: inside that box was *The Gospel of Judas*. Hannah hunted around for possible buyers, quite aware of its value, demanding US$3 million for it. Finally, Geneva-based Greek dealer Nikolas Koutoulakis sent his girlfriend Mia (or was it Effy?) to scope out the situation. Working behind her lover's back, she struck a private deal with Hannah, but too late. The Sneaky Greeky was leagues ahead of his two-timing wench of a girl, and robbed Hannah's home of all manuscripts including the pages of Judas's glory.

He then smuggled them to Geneva, where they were offered for $3,000,000. In the madness of smuggling, theft and deception of sex and religion, Mia had ended up stealing a few of the pages. In the interim, Koutoulakis showed his papyri to fellow Greek antiquities dealer Frieda Tchakos, who was based in Zurich. This was in 1982.

If the cliché is ever appropriate, then here: This is too good to be true! But the story goes on:

In spite of the clearly emaciated manuscript, Hannah is on the lookout further for clientele. Newly recruited evaluators from American elite *Unis* fly in. They should help transfer the discovery over into academic domains. Yet all transactions break down on the price. Even Yale is not willing to come up with such an exorbitant sum.

The dating to 1982 would of course make this encounter prior to the occasion when Steve saw the material in Geneva on May 15, 1983! One may well wonder whether anything can be done with this story other than enjoy it. But we pedantic scholars do look for bits and pieces of information even in such more-or-less fictional stories.

It is of course possible that efforts by the owner to sell to Koutoulakis took place, indeed went so far as to involve Frieda Tchacos, but when they broke down, Perdios approached Koenen on behalf of his friend. But really all that we can know with any certainty about *The Gospel of Judas* in Geneva is the eyewitness report of Steve Emmel:

REPORT ON THE PAPYRUS MANUSCRIPTS OFFERED FOR SALE IN GENEVA, SWITZERLAND, MAY 15, 1983

The collection of papyri being offered for sale consists of four separate manuscripts, and possibly fragments of some others. A system of numeration and designations was agreed upon with the owner and his intermediary for referring to the four manuscripts, as follows:

1. "Exodus" (Greek)
2. "Coptic Apocalypses Codex" (Coptic)
3. "Letters of Paul" (Coptic)
4. "Metrodological Fragment" (Greek)

The material was being stored in three cardboard boxes lined with newspaper. Items 1, 2, and 4 were each in a separate box, with the fragments of item 3 mixed together with items 1 and 4. This report is concerned only with the Coptic items, mainly with item 2, briefly with item 3.

Item 3 is fragments of a papyrus codex from the 5th (possibly 4th) century AD containing at least some of the letters of St. Paul. The leaves are approximately 24 cm tall and 16 cm broad. The scribe outlined his writing area with pink chalk. His handwriting is cursive in style, as though somewhat quickly written. The pages are numbered above the center of a single column of writing, the highest page number observed being 115. There are some nearly complete leaves of the codex preserved, and many smaller fragments, which might be reassembled into at least a sizeable portion of the codex. There is also part of a leather binding (either the front or the back cover, including the spine, lined with scrap papyrus) which probably, though not certainly, belongs to this codex. The contents identified with certainty are Hebrews, Colossians, and 1 Thessalonians. The texts are in a non-standard form of the Sahidic dialect.

Certainly the gem of the entire collection of four manuscripts is item 2, a papyrus codex from the 4th century AD, approximately 30 cm tall and 15 cm broad, containing gnostic texts. At the time that the codex was discovered, it was probably in good condition, with a leather binding and complete leaves with all four margins intact. But the codex has been badly handled; only half of the leather binding (probably the front cover) is now preserved and the leaves have suffered some breakage. The absence of half of the binding and the fact that page numbers run only into the 50's lead me to suppose that the back half of the codex may be missing; only closer study can prove or disprove this supposition. The texts are in a non-standard form of Sahidic.

The codex was inscribed in a single column in a large and careful uncial hand. Page numbers were placed above the center of the column and decorated with short rows of diples [hatch-marks] above and below. At least pp. 1–50 are represented by substantial fragments which, when reassembled, will make up complete leaves with all four margins intact. The portion of the leather binding preserved is lined with cartonnage, layers of scrap papyrus glued together to form a kind of cardboard. At least some of this cartonnage is inscribed, offering hope that the date and location of the manufacture of the codex can be determined with some precision once the cartonnage has been removed and studied.

The codex contains at least three different texts: (1) "The First Apocalypse of James" known already, though in a different version, from Nag Hammadi Codex (NHC) V; (2) "The Letter of Peter to Philip" known already from the NHC VIII (in the new manuscript this title, [in Coptic] TEPISTOLH MPETROS SHAFILIPPOS, is given as a subscript [cf. the superscript title, slightly different, in NHC VIII 132:10–11] accompanied by decorations to fill out the remainder of the page on which the text ends); and (3) a dialogue between Jesus and his disciples (at least "Judas" [i.e., presumably, Judas Thomas] is involved) similar in genre to "The Dialogue of the Savior" (NHC III) and "The Wisdom of Jesus Christ" (NHC III and the Berlin Gnostic codex [PB 8502]).

The leaves and fragments of the codex will need to be conserved between panes of glass. I would recommend conservation measures patterned after those used to restore and conserve the Nag Hammadi Codices (see my article, "The Nag Hammadi Codices Editing Project: A Final Report," American Research Center in Egypt, Inc., *Newsletter* 104 [1978] 10–32). Despite the breakage that has already occurred, and that which will inevitably occur between now and the proper conservation of the manuscript, I estimate that it would require about a month to reassemble the fragments of the manuscript and to arrange the reassembled leaves between panes of glass.

According to the owner, all four of the manuscripts in this collection were found near the village of Beni Masar, about 8 km south of Oxyrhynchus (modern Behnasa). It is difficult to know how seriously to take such information. Study of the cartonnage in the two surviving covers will probably provide more certain information as to the provenance at least of the manufacture of the codices.

The owner asked $3,000,000 for the entire collection. He refused to consider lowering his price to within a reasonable range, claiming that he had already come down from $10,000,000 in negotiations with one previous prospective buyer. He also refused to discuss the prices of the four individual items separately. He would like to sell all four manuscripts together, but probably will sell them individually if necessary.

I strongly urge you to acquire this Gnostic codex. It is of the utmost scholarly value, comparable in every way to any one of the Nag Hammadi Codices. Like them as well, it is one of the oldest specimens of a book in codex form; the fact that part of the cover is also preserved is a remarkable stroke of luck. There is great danger of further deterioration of the manuscript as long as it is in the hands of the present owner. This unique item must be put as quickly as possible into the hands of a library or museum where it can be restored, published, and conserved.

Stephen Emmel
June 1, 1983

FIVE

The Peddling of
The Gospel of Judas

THE SWISS PURCHASE, 1999–2000

In the previous chapter, Dutch-born, London-based Michel Van Rijn's version of the story on his "artnews" Web site ended with Geneva-based art dealer Nikolas Koutoulakis showing the papyrus manuscript of *The Gospel of Judas* to fellow antiquities dealer Frieda Tchacos in 1982. If Tchacos actually saw the codices in 1982, it certainly took a long time for her to act, for the Swiss seem to have acquired the material only in 1999. German journalist Roger Thiede reports on the acquisition, also making the point that Mia (Koutoulakis's devious girlfriend) was involved:[1]

First when the smart attorney Mario Jean Roberty, spokesman of the worldwide-active Basel *"Maecenas Stiftung für antike Kunst"* [Maecenas Foundation for Ancient Art], as well as his client, the business-woman Frieda Nussberger-Tchacos of the Zürich gallery Nefer, take over leading rolls, does the thing get rolling. In 1999 the purchase succeeds, with parts coming from Mia's direction.

Of course this association of Mia with Frieda Nussberger-Tchacos is at least intriguing. The girlfriend of the Greek agent Nikolas Koutoulakis is only referred to as "Mia," which is the feminine of the Greek numeral *one*, and can mean a female *someone*. Just what her real name was and why it is not divulged remain unclear. Perhaps no one ever knew, or cared.

In typically Swiss bilingualism, Ralph Pöhner in his 2005 article in *FACTS* had given the first name of the Zürich businesswoman, in French, as Frédérique,[2] of which Frieda is a Swiss-German abbreviation or nickname. She has a hyphenated last name, which in Switzerland is the proper way for a married couple to give their names: first the last name of the husband, and then, after a hyphen, the maiden name of the wife. Thus, prior to her marriage, her name would seem to have been Frédérique (Frieda) Tchacos. Tchacos is a Greek name. (My Swiss friend and colleague at Harvard Divinity School, François Bovon, assures me that it is neither German nor Swiss dialect.) It is sometimes spelled with *k* (Tcha*k*os), instead of *c* (Tcha*c*os), with the *k* being of course the Greek *kappa*, though often transliterated, as here, with *c*.

Tchacos seems to have been just the right person for the job:[3]

> Behind the Maecenas Foundation façade, the manuscript's real owner is one of the biggest antiquities dealers, Frieda Tchacos (aka Frieda Nussberger). She declined, via Roberty [the Swiss attorney for the Maecenas Foundation], to be interviewed for this article, but is described by London dealers as "very shrewd, very low profile, very smart." Said to be of Greek parentage but brought up in Alexandria, she later moved to Switzerland and has run galleries in Paris and Geneva. "She speaks all the languages, and does business on the highest level; millions and millions of pounds," says one London dealer.

Roberty says the reason Tchacos declines to discuss the manuscript is that, since publicity about the gospel in recent weeks in German and Swiss magazines, Christian fundamentalists have picketed her home in Switzerland, and daubed slogans on its surrounding walls.

Frieda may well have negotiated with Mia in Greek! Of course, whether Frieda ever met Mia is not known. In fact, by this time Mia may have been completely out of the picture (if she ever was in it). After all, she had been involved in a rather wrenching experience (even for the papyrus).

Of course Tchacos could have dealt solely with Nikolas Koutoulakis (no doubt also in Greek . . .), as Michel van Rijn had reported:

Koutoulakis showed his papyri to fellow Greek antiquities dealer Frieda Tchakos.

The Swiss journalist of Zürich, Ralph Pöhner, reports with obvious pride:[4]

Finally in 1999 the Swiss interests take over the batch of documents from the Egyptian [presumably the owner from Cairo named Hannah in the German and Dutch reports, and the unnamed Coptic owner in Steve Emmel's report] . "We have it from him," confirmed Roberty; who the man in Cairo was, the lawyer is not willing to reveal: "We want first to make sure that the Egyptian authorities do not take legal proceedings against him for exporting cultural materials."

Quite recently, Roberty has clarified the awkward situation in which the Egyptian from whom it was purchased finds himself:[5]

You see, the problem we have with Egypt (to whom the codex will be donated) is that their system of law is quite different from ours. There is not a real reliability. So we prefer, and in the publication many names of Egyptian nationals will be—not omitted—and we will use different names.

Asked whether the seller would be prosecuted under Egyptian law, he replied: "No. The statutes of limitation have already passed." But he explained that the problem lies elsewhere:

People in the country may think these people have become extremely wealthy and there are many risks that we wouldn't want the people running into.

All the real names will be deposited, so that on the scholarly level there will be full transparency.

Legally speaking there are no risks. It is absolutely clean and transparent if it will be accepted as such, but in that country, with which I've had other experiences, you never exactly know how things are handled.

If they stick to certain rules, it will mostly be harassment. Through the lapse of time most people have become very elderly, and I don't think they deserve being harassed much.

Van Rijn reports that Tchacos had succeeded in reuniting what Mia had stolen and what Hannah had retained or recuperated:[6]

In the summer of 1999, Frieda had come across some stolen papyrus that she thought to be Mia's. She then traveled to Cairo in November, where she discussed the purchase of the full manuscript with Hannah. Hannah had put the Gospel in a rusty safe-deposit box in a Citibank in Hicksville, New York. She flew out to see it and purchased it soon after for an unknown sum.

Pöhner had said Tchacos acquired the material in 1999 from the unnamed Copt, Hannah. But Thiede mentions Hannah's parts only in 2000, when the "parts coming from Mia's direction" are united with the rest:[7]

In the year 2000 Frieda Nussberger[-Tchacos] achieved the reuniting of the treasure with those parts that Hannah had meanwhile deposited in the basement of the Citibank of Hicksville, New York.

Tchacos no doubt speaks German and its Swiss dialect in Zürich, French in Paris and Geneva, Greek in Athens, Arabic in Cairo, and English in New York. It is indeed useful that "she speaks all the languages."

YALE UNIVERSITY

Tchacos turned to Yale University as a potential purchaser:[8]

At first it seemed unclear how one should precede with the find. In the year 2000 the Zürich art dealer Frédérique Nussberger—client of Roberty—arrived with the documents at the Beinecke Library of Yale University. Again it comes to no settlement. "We renounced the purchase," says the curator of the library, Robert Babcock. "The reasons we do not discuss publicly." Only this much: "The genuineness was not the issue—we considered it to be authentic."

Harry Attridge was involved in the assessment at Yale, and submitted to me the following report:

At Yale, the curator of ancient manuscripts in the Beinecke Library, Dr. Robert Babcock, invited Bentley Layton and me to have a look at the Coptic Codex and to give him our judgment about its probable significance. I believe that he was interested in acquiring the whole find. Since his area is Greek papyrology, he would have been in a position to make a judgment about the value and significance of the Greek material that was also part of the offering. I don't recall him discussing the price being asked for the materials—such discretion would be pretty standard—, nor did he identify the seller or his agent. We had no contact with either seller or agent. We had brief access to the Coptic codex itself in offices of the Beinecke Library and were able to verify that it did indeed appear to be what we had heard about from Steve Emmel, a codex, probably of the 4th–5th century in a decent literary hand not unlike that of the Nag Hammadi codices. We did not have time to read or transcribe the texts in the codex, nor, to my recollection, did we discuss the possible identification of the text as a *Gospel of Judas.* I was not involved in the decision not to acquire the materials, which was made by the staff of the Beinecke, but I'm not sure at what level.

TCHACOS AND FERRINI: CONTRACT
OF SEPTEMBER 9, 2000

The manuscripts are next attested on September 9, 2000, where one finds on the Internet[9] a contract signed on that date. It is between "Frieda Nussberger Tchacos, whose address is Augustinergasse 14, 8001 Zurich, Switzerland (hereinafter referred to as 'Seller')" and "Nemo, LLC, whose address is 1080 Top of the Hill Road, Akron, Ohio (hereinafter referred to as 'Buyer')." The buyer can be identified as Bruce Ferrini. The purchase price, to be paid in installments without interest, is $1,500,000, half "on or before January 15, 2001, and the other half "on or before February 15, 2001." The contract states:

> The Manuscript was, in all regards, legally exported from the country of its origin and has been legally exported from and imported into all countries through which it has passed, including the United States.

> No person or entity is in possession of any copy, photograph, facsimile or reproduction by any means or in any medium of the Manuscript or the text thereof.

> . . . because Seller acquired and took delivery of the Manuscript in the United States, it does not possess and shall not be required to deliver hereafter any export or import licenses.

The contract is signed by Bruce Ferrini, Pres., Nemo, LLC, as Buyer, and Frieda Nussberger Tchacos, as Seller.

MARTIN SCHØYEN: SEPTEMBER 11, 2000

Ferrini promptly went to work to see if he could sell the manuscripts for more than he would have to pay for them. He offered them to one of his clients, Martin Schøyen, perhaps knowing that it is he who had earlier shown an interest in acquiring them. On September 11, 2000, he received the following response from Schøyen, who makes his own appraisals on the basis of the sale price of comparable materials at auctions:[10]

The following prices were stipulated, and consented to by Hannah more or less, for the meeting in N. Y. 12th–13 Dec. 1990 (cancelled due to "Desert Storm"):

1. Exodus, 4th c. More than 50 ff. Greek	$365,000
2. 3 Gnostic texts, Coptic 25 ff.+10? in fragments, 4th (incl. 1 cover)	281,000
3. Letters of Paul (3 epistles), Coptic, ca. 400, 30ff. (incl. 1 cover & spine)	252,000
4. Mathematical, 5th c. 12 ff.?	88,000
	$986,000

For no. 2 an addition was made of 10%, since 1 of the covers was preserved, and for no. 3 +15% for 1 cover & the spine of the binding (are these present?) . . .

You should check whether everything is still present: (2 binding covers/spine about 12 ff. Mathematical (distinctive cursive script) and Letters of Paul (part of Colossians, 1st Thessalonians and Hebrews).

Schøyen had at the time made such calculations, based on his familiarity with the antiquities market, and had sent them to me. But there was no response from the owner, so that his comment to Ferrini that the prices were "more or less consented to by Hannah" would have to be emphasized on the side of "less."[11] In effect, Schöyen was informing Ferrini what he was willing to pay as a fair price. It did not come to enough for Ferrini to be able to pay Frieda her asking price, much less to make a profit. So the sale to Schøyen did not take place, I am sorry to say.

CHARLES W. HEDRICK

Charlie Hedrick had been consulted by Ferrini from time to time about ancient manuscripts that Ferrini had access to in his business, asking Hedrick to identify them for him from photographs he would send. On February 6, 2001, Roberty e-mailed the following to van Rijn, having heard from him about the involvement of Hedrick in the present case:

> Charlie's contribution really surprises me. I had no idea of his theological background being as solid on such a particular subject. This kind as well as any other kind of contributions or revelations of facts I can't possibly be aware of, would make your update extremely more helpful—for the benefit of the cause . . . !

I of course welcome Hedrick's education being called "solid," since, after all, I was his doctoral father! He is today Distinguished Emeritus Professor of Religious Studies at Missouri State University.

Hedrick received from Bruce Ferrini 164 "very dismal digital photographs," where he could at least identify *James* from the title of *The (First) Apocalypse of James* and the title of *The Letter of Peter to Philip*,[12] which Steve Emmel had already identified in Geneva, and which have been mentioned in the current publicity about *The Gospel of Judas* as included in what has returned to Switzerland.[13] He also received ten professionally made photographs and twenty-four made with a regular camera. Hedrick transcribed and translated what he could from six pages that were more nearly legible. The difficulty was twofold: the papyrus itself was quite damaged, more so than when Steve Emmel had seen the leaves in 1983, especially in that the top third of many leaves were now missing. Emmel had seen the pagination in the top margin, which was no longer available to Hedrick to help put the photographs in their correct sequence. And also when the bottom of one page and the top of the next are extant, one can establish the sequence of leaves by following the train of thought, which unfortunately was no longer possible.

Hedrick circulated his transcriptions and translations to the circle of colleagues who had worked together over the years on the Nag Hammadi Codices, Birger A. Pearson, John D. Turner, Douglas M. Parrott, Wolf-Peter Funk, Hans-Gebhard Bethge, and me, and received from most a series of suggestions for improving both the transcription and the translation. The outcome of this collaboration has been, most recently, a much improved transcription and German translation by the group in Berlin led by Bethge, and a corresponding English translation by Steven Patterson. The last page of the text reads as follows:

> They made sure that they seized him during the prayer.
> For they were afraid of the people, because he was in all
> their hands as a prophet. And they approached Judas.
> They said to him: What are you doing in this place? Aren't
> you a disciple of Jesus? But he answered them according
> to their wishes. But Judas took some money. He deliv-
> ered him over to them.
> #### The Gospel
> #### of Judas

It is to be much regretted that this familiar kind of collegial sharing and cooperation, characteristic of the study of Nag Hammadi by those not part of the Nag Hammadi monopolies, has not been shared, in the case of *The Gospel of Judas*, by those who have—a monopoly on it!

Hedrick published reports of his photographs of *The Gospel of Judas* in 2002 and 2003 in the scholarly journals *Bible Review* and *Journal of Early Christian Studies*:[14]

> In sum, in addition to the four canonical gospels, we have four complete noncanonicals, seven fragmentary, four known from quotations and two hypothetically recovered for a total of 21 gospels from the first two centuries, and we know that others existed in the early period. I am confident more of them will be found. For example, I have seen photos of several pages from a Coptic text entitled *The Gospel of Judas* that recently surfaced on the antiquities market.

> One of those gospels generally thought to have disappeared, the gospel of Judas (known to Irenaeus toward the end of the second century), actually did survive in Coptic translation, and has been available on the antiquities market for several years.

This too was picked up by the Swiss reporter Pöhner:[15]

> In June 2002 the *Bible Review* reported about the photographs circulating on the manuscript market, as did in November 2003 the *Journal of Early Christian Studies*. It has to do with securing an important document for humanity. Already previously Michel van Rijn picked up the theme: The former art smuggler, who presents himself as a warrant officer, and illumines the cloudy side of the art market, reports on his web site that a *Gospel of Judas* is on the market. "Don't touch," he warns.

Similarly Roger Thiede picked up the trail of Hedrick, and indeed identified the fact that Hedrick himself had discovered

and edited one of the noncanonical gospels that has appeared
in recent times:[16]

> Then rumors circulate in uni[versity] circles about the
> true content of the most voluminous part of the codex.
> Charles W. Hedrick, Professor at Southwest Missouri
> State University, goes public. Together with his colleague
> Paul Mirecki, he had become world famous in 1997 by
> making known "Papyrus Berolinensis 22220."[17] In the
> archives of the Egyptian Museum of the German capi-
> tal the pair had dredged up remains of a Coptic Gospel
> fragment (see *FOCUS*, fascicle 14 of 1997), in Hedrick's
> numeration "E 34." Now the same scholar gave in evi-
> dence, in the scholarly journal *Bible Review*, that he had
> seen fotos of pages of a further, very important writing.
> "E 35" is for the first time spoken about publicly.

ROBERTY'S MEMORANDUM: DECEMBER 15, 2000

The contract signed by Ferrini and Tchacos was not implemented, because on December 15, 2000, Roberty, as a Swiss
attorney, wrote a memorandum to a New York attorney, Eric
R. Kaufman, who had been their host at a recent meeting of
the two lawyers with "Frieda" and "Bruce," presumably their
respective clients.[18] The memorandum itemizes the agreements reached by "Frieda" and "Bruce" "under somewhat
tensed circumstances" at that meeting. It begins by stating
that the agreements of September 9, 2000, "have become obso-
lete."

Since, according to the memorandum, Bruce had "already
disposed of" the Mathematical Treatise and Letters of Paul, he
would pay Frieda $300,000 for them by February 1, 2001. With
regard to the rest of the manuscripts, a foundation would be
created to carry out the "project":

The entity which shall realize the Project shouldn't be a commercial entity but the *Logos Foundation* as officially recognized charitable trust of public utility to be established under Swiss Law soon.

11. . . . Moreover, the actual owner of the manuscripts [Frieda] intends to make a partial donation of the manuscripts to the Foundation whereby all rights to the manuscripts as well as deriving from the manuscripts shall be transferred to the *Logos Foundation* against assignment of totally 80 % of the Foundation's future revenues from the commercialization of the manuscripts (i.e. from the exploitation of the deriving publishing rights etc. and ultimately—if legally admissible—from their sale).

Bruce and Frieda are going to exchange the composite volume of at least three Coptic texts (*First Apocalypse of James, Epistle of Peter to Philip* and *Gospel of Judas*) as well as the Book of Exodus and the not expressly mentioned further fragments with two checks emitted by Bruce of USD 1,250,000—each, the first due on January 15, 2001 and the second due on February 15, 2001.

Immediately after the above described exchange has taken place, Frieda will set up the *Logos Foundation* in agreement with you and in accordance with the above described principles. She will then transfer the manuscripts to the Foundation entering into an agreement as described sub par. 11. above.

Frieda will grant Bruce the option of acquiring half the rights assigned to her by the Foundation to the future revenues from the commercialization of the manuscripts against payment to her of USD 1,100,000 . . . (i.e. USD 750,000—corresponding to half the value of

the composite volume plus USD 350,000—corresponding to half the value of the Book of Exodus) and against
donation to the Foundation of the same amounts she
will have donated herself by then. This option shall be
valid and exercisable until June 30, 2001.

The purpose of the proposed Logos Foundation was stated as
follows:

> The *Logos Project* intends to save and publish *The Gos-
> pel of Judas* and other related manuscripts for the benefit
> of historical truth and to generate the funds necessary for
> this task as well as for the compensation of the expenses
> and efforts incurred by the promoters, leaving them with
> a decent profit.

The agreement reached in New York also imposed the strictest
secrecy, which seems to have been handed down at each stage
of the project until now.

> It is clearly understood by all persons involved that
> nobody, not even Bruce and Frieda, but only the Foun-
> dation, will have the right to promulgate and commer-
> cialize any knowledge regarding, concerning or deriving
> from the manuscripts. Moreover, for the time being and
> until all legal aspects are clarified, it is in the best inter-
> est of the Project to maintain utmost secrecy about its
> existence.

This leaves only Roberty the freedom to discuss whatever he
wants with whomever he wants, and he has apparently made
great use of this freedom.

Apparently Ferrini did not accept the offer to share in the
income from the commercialization of the manuscripts to be

owned by a new Foundation. Subsequently, his name nowhere figures in connection with the Foundation.

It is presumably the projected Logos Foundation that came into existence under the name of the Maecenas Foundation, the current owner of *The Gospel of Judas.*

BREAKING NEWS . . . "BRUCE ON THE LOOSE"

Michel van Rijn reports on what happened following the meeting in New York.[19] Van Rijn and Roberty had worked together cordially in earlier connections, and therefore Van Rijn had notified Roberty of the news on *The Gospel of Judas* he was about to publish on his Web site. Van Rijn then published what was apparently Roberty's revised draft of what Van Rijn had e-mailed him for approval, since it begins: "Michel, what do you think about the following text?"

> Crime against Humanity . . . Priceless and not replaceable *Gospel of Judas* embezzled by manuscript dealer Bruce P. Ferrini (http://www.ferrini.com)
>
> The mechanics:
>
> Last fall, Zurich based antiques dealer Frieda Chakos entrusts priceless papyrus manuscripts which had been in a Bank vault in New York for almost 20 years to the "safe" facilities of Akron/Ohio-based manuscript dealer Bruce P. Ferrini. She is approached by Ferrini through a middleman and doesn't have a clue that by this time Ferrini is already in deep financial troubles. The news had not hit the papers yet. Ferrini takes advantage of the secrecy of the art-market and offers to help Frieda 'in preserving these manuscripts for the benefit of mankind'. . .
>
> The papyrus manuscripts consist of

- a Gnostic codex in Sahidic dialect containing the lost *Gospel of Judas* known from history only through Saint Irenaeus (c. 140–202 AD), Bishop of Lyon, *The First Apocalypse of James* and *The Epistle of Peter to Philip*
- the *Book of Exodus* in Greek
- *Letters of Paul* in Sahidic dialect and a
- *Mathematical Treatise* in Greek.

All these manuscripts are priceless historical documents, only comparable to major finds like the Nag Hammadi Library or the Dead Sea Scrolls from Qumran. They belong to mankind and shall be publicly preserved and studied. For this purpose, Frieda has set up a public foundation to which these manuscripts have been donated. But Ferrini wants to turn them into money for the satisfaction of his greedy ambitions and has therefore spirited the manuscripts away, to Japan.

Legal proceedings and criminal persecution are under way. This will take some time. As things develop, you will see how much more efficient I am with my DEVASTATING ART NEWS. Crimes against the most basic cultural interests of mankind must be persecuted by adequate means. Buyers beware, a maniac dealer is selling parts of our history. You buy? You touch? You will be prosecuted!

On February 5, 2001, Roberty again e-mailed van Rijn:

Let me quickly tell you what really has happened: Basically nothing. Last Monday night (Jan 29) Eric K[aufman] called several times and repeatedly confirmed he didn't know what this fuss was all about because his client was perfectly willing to return the manuscripts (exception for "The Mathematical Treatise" and "The Letters of Paul" which he has already sold and for which he should have paid $300 on Feb 1) as soon as [he] would be returning to Akron on Feb 14, back from the Palm Beach Antiques Fair (or from Japan?). Since these phone calls I (or Frieda) have received no further communication either from Eric or from the Italo-Sioux [Ferrini] himself. Tomorrow, we can check the bank for the arrival of $300 as promised!? Of course, I know Eric had been absent Tue and Wed and he knew I was going to Paris until Fri night.

The point is, I would like to keep the pressure on B.F. until he really fulfills his (lawyer's) promise. Therefore, probably the best and only possible update on "Bruce on the Loose" is the naked truth: Thanks to "Devastating Art News" promising contacts have been established between the lawyers of the parties involved and hopefully B.F. will keep his (lawyer's) word and have the manuscripts returned by February 14/15, 2001.

Then on February 7, 2001, Roberty e-mailed van Rijn still another time:

Now I know you don't only have a third ear but also a third eye: Yesterday, just before leaving for the meeting with Eric, I checked my mailbox and got your prophetical message about what Eric would be saying and proposing. You were right to the dot!

I still don't quite get what Bruce really wants—besides trying to make the business of his life, i.e. selling manuscripts (letters of Paul and Mathematical Treatise) as well as some objects of art and exploiting and possibly selling the important manuscripts without ever having to pay for them. It's the precise attitude of a professional embezzler and thief . . .

During our meeting, there were three major issues:

- who is passing information on to you
- the overdue payment of USD 300" for the manu[script]s already sold
- the refusal to return the other manu[script]s.

1. In order to figure out where the leak is, Eric suggested Bruce to feed three different, false infos to three different possible leaks. Watch out!

2. The overdue payment has been done because of a confusion with dealings Bruce has with Bill Veres. Bill claims Bruce [is] owing him money and pretends having paid Frieda on behalf on Bruce USD 90" (which is not true!) and Bruce claims Bill [is] owing him lots of money. Bill had introduced Bruce to Frieda and pretends to be his partner. At the same time he pretends feeling responsible towards Frieda for the mess she is in. For reasons completely independent of Bruce, Bill owes Frieda about USD 150". All this confusion is basically bullshit and is being used by Bruce just to avoid payment. By the way, he pretends that the sales price obtained by Sam Fogg is not of USD 900" and that the sale was not to Thompson.

3. Because in your latest update you claim having been asked for assistance by the Egyptian authorities, Eric pretends Bruce being no longer able to return the manu[script]s without risking persecution under US law! This is pure bullshit again and he would have brought this same argument even if you had not mentioned the Egyptian authorities. From what I have learned and seen documented, I can affirm that following legal terms (the applicable Egyptian law being No. 215 of October 31, 1951) there is no possibility for a claim from that coun-

try. Of course, this does not foreclose some action out of purely political motives . . .

We are now considering the remaining options. Possibly, there will be another meeting on Friday afternoon with Bruce present.

I'll keep you posted.

Apparently the Maecenas Foundation, whose only purpose is to commercialize *The Gospel of Judas* and the other less sensational texts, had a rough start, if it could not get hold of the manuscripts themselves. What actually transpired (Japan? legal proceedings?) is not clear, but the manuscripts did finally come into the possession of the newly created Maecenas Foundation.

How long it all took is not clear. There is a comment by Thiede, suggesting that it dragged on into 2002:[20]

In 2002 she plans again to dismember the codex. For twice $750,000 it is to go to the US dealer Bruce Ferrini of Akron, Ohio. Nothing comes of this. Instead, Maecenas is soon to be recognized as the new owner of the badly handled ruin of a book.

The only thing this odd comment by Thiede seems to have in common with the agreement reached in New York is the evaluation of the Gnostic composite codex at twice $750,000, i.e., a total value of $1,500,000. It may be that part of the legal pressure on Ferrini took the form that he was either to pay cash for buying the manuscripts or return them to Roberty. Since he was in financial straits, he finally returned them.

"BAD PROVENANCE": ILLEGAL
EXCAVATION AND SMUGGLING

Michel van Rijn claims credit for exposing the illegal exportation of *The Gospel of Judas* from Egypt, which hence necessitated the agreement by the Maecenas Foundation to return it to Egypt after publication. But this did not take place automatically, as Van Rijn explains with grim satisfaction:[21]

> Zürich based dealer Frieda (Nussberger) Chakos, owner of the prestigious Gallery Nefer, is up to her old tricks again. Although she solemnly promised, after being exposed on my website, to return the illegally acquired, historically invaluable *Gospel of Judas* to Egypt, she is presently negotiating a possible sale to a US manuscript dealer. We are on the job as usual and will keep you posted. If Frieda will go forward, we will also dive into her past sales and rip the last bits of her already miserable reputation to pieces.

Later, Van Rijn follows up with his success story:[22]

> In 2001 this portal first revealed the existence and the contents of the looted *Judas Gospel* as well as enough of the skullduggery in its recent history to make it unmarketable. The action on this portal forced the culprits who owned the long lost smuggled Gospel to restore it to its true country of origin, Egypt, and to look for other venues to capitalize on their illegally acquired treasure. This portal is used to not being credited in the media for the good work we do . . . and we take consolation and soulage in the fact that as a result of our actions this historically important document will be returned to Egypt safe for posterity.

Van Rijn prides himself on his art-world scoops, and it was on his website that news of the existence of an extraordinary document first broke—at least beyond the cabals of dealers, and the cloistered confines of the scholarly community. In 2001, he revealed that the long-lost *Gospel of Judas* Iscariot—not seen for at least 1,800 years—was being hawked around antiquities dealers on two, maybe three, continents. It wasn't quite the Dead Sea Scrolls, but not far off. Would this testament of Judas, the betrayer of Jesus, turn Christianity on its head? Van Rijn says it asserts that Judas worked in league with Jesus to betray him, thereby to ensure his crucifixion, martyrdom (and, for believers, his resurrection), and thus to lay the foundation for—and ensure the success of— Christianity. "Forget *The Da Vinci Code*, says Van Rijn. This is the real deal."

The outcome, of course, has been a rupture in the good relations that had prevailed between Van Rijn and Roberty (who had even functioned as his Van Rijn's representative), according to Malcolm Macalister Hall's report in the British newspaper *The Independent*:[23]

But few allegiances last long in the quicksand of the antiquities market, and the two now have daggers drawn. "Van Rijn and Roberty—it's like Holmes and Moriarty; they're mortal enemies," says one major London dealer. In this feud, Van Rijn has done all he can to discredit the provenance of *The Gospel of Judas*—all part of his plan, he says, to make it unsellable. He's now cock-a-hoop that the Maecenas Foundation has pledged to return the manuscript to Egypt—to the Coptic Museum in Cairo—after unsuccessful attempts to sell it and other papyri in the United States for some $2.5m. Van Rijn claims that his website postings over the last few years destroyed any possible deal.

Roberty's memorandum of December 15, 2000, did name the original owner in a clause questioning the legal title:

> In order to be able to pursue the Project responsibly, we first must ascertain that Mr. Hana A. Airian had obtained good legal and beneficial title to the manuscripts and that he had the right to sell these documents to Frieda.

Since no such legal title was forthcoming, this could have been used by Ferrini as a reason/excuse for not going forward, as Dutch journalist Henk Schutten has reported:[24]

> The big question is why this manuscript remained hidden for such a long time after it was discovered. Almost no one wanted to get their fingers burned, according to Bruce Ferrini, an art dealer of Akron, Ohio. He himself was offered the documents in 2000 by Frieda Tchakos, a gallery owner in Geneva who bought the materials the year prior to that. . . .
>
> The problem was the "bad provenance," its obscure origin. Tchakos and Roberty told Ferrini that farmers discovered the books in the mid-seventies in a stone box in Megaga, Upper-Egypt. . . .
>
> Ferrini: "Frieda told me that the documents were obtained by a Greek trader, Nikolas Koutoulakis who had supposedly stolen them from Hannah, an Egyptian jeweler. Koutoulakis smuggled them into Geneva. Frieda alleges that Hannah followed him by traveling to Geneva to reclaim the documents. A Coptic priest would have accompanied Hannah afterwards to New York where the documents were held in a safe in Hicksville's Citibank.

They remained there until the end of the nineties when they were purchased by Frieda."

The "bad provenance" may well have been one reason that had prevented the agreement of September 19, 2000, from being implemented, since that agreement had stipulated that the title was clear.

The problem of smuggling may also help explain a cryptic comment by Thiede:[25]

Who finally paid what to whom, not even the expert on connections who lives in London, the 54-year-old Michel van Rijn, knows. His rude internet service "artnews" (Motto: "Hot Art Cold Cash") otherwise has its profile with constantly new exposure stories, as the "nemesis" of international art racketeers.

Nonetheless his website suggests sufficiently that for Nussberger a juristic coup was successful. Many-years-long business dealings with an imprisoned art mafioso of the Nile scene should be forgiven and forgotten. Madame is to receive a whitewashing certificate that protects her from Egyptian persecution because of illegal art exports.

Whether, in order to achieve this, Nussberger or Maecenas had to deliver the promise to give her book back formally to Egypt? To be sure, corresponding commitments in a publication of the foundation are formulated in a very airy way.

Similar reports are given by Michel Van Rijn:[26]

Present "owner"—Zurich-based Frieda Nussberger Tchakos —struck a deal with the Egyptian government, under which she was absolved of looting that nation clean. But, unlike Judas, she held out for a bit more than 30 pieces of silver. After all, Frieda was one of Tarek El-Sweissi's [Egyptian official convicted in 2003 of smuggling ancient artifacts out of Egypt] principal dealers, the latter, of course, sweating in a hot Egyptian cell for the next 30 years.

This then would tend to put in question the lofty ideals used to explain the commitment to return the manuscripts to Egypt.

COMMERCIALIZING *THE GOSPEL OF JUDAS*

The fact that the manuscript could not be sold for a profit, but rather has to be returned to Egypt, made the commercializing of the contents of *The Gospel of Judas* the chosen path to riches. Roger Thiede explains:[27]

> Clearly the Swiss now see their salvation in the rapid journalistic marketing of the codex. One lets it be known that the careful restoration has been turned over to the best experts. As scholarly editor, the dean of Coptic-Sahidic literature, the Geneva Professor Emeritus Rodolphe Kasser, the uncontested star of the discipline had been enlisted.

It is apparently due to this strategy of making big money from sensationalizing the text, if not from selling the papyrus itself, that the matter should be kept a secret until the moment of its publication arrives, rather than the suspense being broken by the contents being leaked to the press:[28]

> **Further inquiries pointless.** For the rest, one stays covered. The Zürich art dealership Nefer at present no longer exists. Even friendly gallery people do not know where the ex-owner is hiding. But she still has the threads in hand. In any case, that is certified by experts who are commissioned as scholarly coworkers of the first edition,

yet they cannot give information because of a prohibition to speak out.

Tiede explains:[29]

> Precisely because the "new" text—due to its risky substance—is still unpublished, and Maecenas/Roberty likes to identify only the last page (circulating in the internet) as an original part of his manuscript, the discussion meanwhile overflows.

By way of identifying Roberty, Thiede elaborates:[30]

> The Judas manuscript belongs, after the transactions of the most recent past, to the Swiss "*Maecenas Stiftung für antike Kunst.*" It supports archeological excavations and advises in museum construction. The institution is led by the Basel attorney Mario Jean Roberty, who appeared already in numerous cultural events. He was attorney of the Japanese Miho museum and contrived the transfer of antiquities back into Egypt. His restrictive politics on information with regard to the Judas book is severely criticized.

THE DETERIORATING CONDITION OF THE DISCOVERY

The convoluted story of the peddling of *The Gospel of Judas* is full of intrigue, greed, and drama as the text is passed through many hands and across many borders. But such peregrinations have taken their toll on the ancient papyrus manuscript.

The size of the original fourth-century codex, the number of leaves it originally contained, is of course quite a different question from the number of leaves that survive today, though the two tend at times to be confused. Let's begin with the number of leaves that are thought to have survived, and only then turn to the number of leaves in the original codex, and how many leaves may have been used to copy out *The Gospel of Judas*, to estimate the tractate's original length as twice that many pages (two *pages* are on the front and back of one *leaf*).

Of course there are different ways to count the number of extant leaves in a very fragmentary codex. When does a *fragment* become honored with the designation of being a *leaf*? The policy might be, for example, that, if over half a leaf is extant, we should no longer call it a *fragment*, but rather call it a *leaf*. But in some of the transcriptions and translations that have been circulating privately among scholars, there may be a "page" transcribed with parts of only eight lines extant. Neither the beginning nor the end of the lines is extant, but only a middle section. This *fragment* or *leaf* is hardly more than an inch high and an inch wide. A few words may be recognized in the extant letters, but there is no coherent sentence that conveys meaning. If a word such as *Jesus*, or *Judas*, or *Allogenes*, is legible, fine! But one is not often so lucky. So: Is this a *fragment*, or is it a *leaf*? In terms of what has survived, it may be more documentation for a leaf that did not survive, than it is a surviving leaf in its own right. If the some thirty "leaves" in the Gnostic codex were all like this, we might as well forget it! Fortunately, some, hopefully most, are much more nearly complete. But one must be warned of the problem inherent in a simple list of how many "leaves" are extant.

The point of departure for any estimate can only be based on Steve Emmel's report cited in chapter four:

> The absence of half of the binding and the fact that page numbers run only into the 50's lead me to suppose that the back half of the codex may be missing; only closer study can prove or disprove this supposition. . . . Page numbers were placed above the center of the column and decorated with short rows of diples above and below. At

least pp. 1–50 are represented by substantial fragments which, when reassembled, will make up complete leaves with all four margins intact.

Schutten reports Emmel as saying:[31]

> The numbers of the pages went up to sixty, while most papyrus codices are at least twice as big. I suspected half of the manuscript to be missing.

Emmel was of course thinking of the Nag Hammadi Codices, where a good number of them have over one hundred pages.

Ferrini indicates that by this time some leaves had been removed from the lot for individual sale, so that Emmel's estimate of 1983 does not apply to the present state of the manuscript:[32]

> Ferrini suspects that in the meantime several single pages of the manuscript were put on the market. "When I saw the work for the first time in 1999, only 25 pages remained intact, so at least half of them were missing. I cannot be absolutely sure if the manuscript was found incomplete or if its writing was never finished. But from time to time new pages would appear. Five or six different documents in total without page numbers, it was just a mess."

There is also the report of Mia being responsible for some loss. Thiede had said:

> Large parts land in Mia's purse, and then evaporate for a long time. One folio leaf is lost forever.

Van Rijn paraphrased: "Mia had ended up stealing a few of the pages." (One does not know whether to believe such details in these more sensational reconstructions of the story.)

Hedrick reported an alarming detail about fragments:[33]

> He [Ferrini] did tell me that he had paid for the codex and then when the provenance was in question that he called his money back in and returned the codex to whoever was selling it to him . . . , and the individual became angry and slammed the codex down on the table and tiny pieces of papyrus flew all over the place. The seller picked up the codex and left angrily saying well maybe I will just burn it.

Hedrick later clarifies this important detail:[34]

> My understanding is that the person who slammed the book on the table was not Frieda, but no names were used. Frieda would not have threatened to burn the book when her price was not met, I do not think.

I agree with Hedrick that Frieda is far too good a businessperson to burn something worth big money. But she may also be a good enough businessperson to make such dramatic statements during ongoing negotiations!

Regarding page numbers at the top of leaves, Hedrick reports from his photographs:[35]

> I do not have the top of the last page of Judas and hence I do not have a page number. . . . There is a top of which I can read "60."

But the number of extant *leaves* may well have been fewer that the highest *page* number that was observed. Hedrick reports:[36]

> At one point I heard that there were only 50 pages in the entire codex (per Ferrini).

This statement from Hedrick may serve to correct the report of Schutten, quoted above, that Ferrini said there were only twenty-five pages left. Perhaps this is to be understood as the frequent confusion between *leaf,* a piece of papyrus with two sides and hence two *pages* of a book, and *page,* which refers to only one side of a *leaf.* Ferrini may have counted twenty-five *leaves* and correctly inferred that this meant fifty *pages,* which he reported to Hedrick.

And yet Schutten continued his report on Ferrini by quoting: "so at least half of them were missing." This suggests that Schutten took Ferrini to be speaking, after all, of pages rather than leaves, from fifty pages down to twenty-five pages. (Could this be a confusion with Emmel's report? Schutten had reported Emmel saying that "the pages went up to sixty" but that Emmel suspected "half of the manuscript to be missing." Of course Emmel meant that the codex may well have had 120 pages originally, but that only half, "up to sixty," were still extant. Schutten may have reconciled the two reports as best he could, but inaccurately.) Of course this remains speculation. All that seems clear is that Ferrini thought the total seen by Emmel had shrunk appreciably.

Hedrick reports in terms of what he could see on the photographs he received from Ferrini:[37]

You must think in terms of jumbled mess. There is only one stack (not two if you had a neat book and the book were opened with some leaves on left and right). The top with the page number has leaves behind it, but because of the breaks in the stack (the breaks seem to go completely through the stack) and because of the jumbled character of the stack, it is not possible to tell which top goes with which of the two pieces of papyrus in the two bottom breaks. The text cannot be read from my poor digital photographs except for the occasional letter, and reading fibers is impossible. There are definitely tops however.

He clarifies still further:[38]

> There is only one stack of leaves one on top of the other. I see three breaks in the stack. One about two-thirds of the way up and then the top third has a break. There are tops of some pages in the stack and the Coptic page number 60 is clearly distinct. (I found no other page numbers.)

Of course Hedrick's parenthetic comment that "the breaks seem to go completely through the stack" suggests the kind of wrenching experience associated with Mia, when the personages in the story more or less literally fought over the codex, and may well have broken it literally in two (or four)!

Hedrick was asked by Kasser to turn over his photographs to him, in hopes of finding there material that he was missing in the papyri themselves. Hedrick reports:[39]

> Kasser was talking about material missing completely from the material he had. He specifically asked me about three bottoms of pages he identified among the photographs I sent him that he did not have among the extant papyrus material in his possession. I suspected, however, he was also concerned about tops of pages.

SIXTY-TWO EXTANT PAGES?

Pöhner wrote that "the book contains 62 pages."[40] Thiede published a photograph of the page with the subscript title *The Gospel of Judas* clearly visible, with the caption for the photograph:[41]

In the manuscript of p. 62 at the end, placed one under the other the designation of the title: "Gospel" and "Judas." The foto circulating in the World Wide Web shows, **according to the information of the owner of the codex,** the last page of the manuscript that is in his possession."

Then Hedrick's provisional draft translation of that page is translated into German, with this caption:[42]

Not all letters of p. 62 are to be deciphered; text according to C. Hedrick.

How does he know that it is "p. 62"? Or, putting the question more carefully (since it probably isn't p. 62): Where does the figure 62 come from? Possibly: if one takes literally the comment "one folio leaf is lost forever," and follows Thiede's chronology, to the effect that the juicy story preceded the visit of "evaluators from American elite *Unis* [universities]," then one might assume that two more pages than those seen by Emmel would have originally been involved. If then one takes literally Schutten's version of Emmel's memory, "up to sixty," rather than Emmel's written report, "at least pp. 1–50 are represented by substantial fragments," one could postulate (probably inaccurately) that there were, when Emmel saw them, in fact sixty pages, plus the two pages already lost in the fray. In this way one reaches a total of sixty-two pages. If then the title *The Gospel of Judas* is on the last page, that last page would be p. 62. *Voila!* One arrives at the pagination listed (very probably incorrectly) by Pöhner and Thiede! And then they seem to assume that this page number can apply as well to the number of extant pages.

Such a calculation would of course not have been made by a careful scholar. For Emmel did not literally count sixty pages.

The tattered papyrus leaves were too fragile for him to thumb through and count thirty leaves. Did someone else actually count the sixty-two pages? Or did Pöhner just assume that two pages had been removed, on the basis of the story that Thiede tells, and add two to Schutten's comment "up to sixty"? This may be only a garbled version of Emmel's report to Schutten, but in any case Emmel did not mean to be exact. He is a very exacting person, and would have made an exact statement if he had had an exact figure. Furthermore, a problem with this explanation of "p. 62" is that Thiede published his article later than did Pöhner!

Hedrick did find a reference to the page number "60" in the top margin of a page. But since the page with the title *The Gospel of Judas* does not have the top margin, it is hard to imagine that the immediately preceding leaf does have the top margin with the pagination 59–60. Usually leaves near each other have a similar profile of damage and deterioration. For this reason, the page with the pagination 60 was probably not immediately under the leaf with the top missing, but with the title *The Gospel of Judas* visible at the bottom of the page.

Of course anything is possible, when one has no concrete information. But in any case one should not refer to pagination in connection with the title of *The Gospel of Judas*. And the page number "60," much less an invented pagination "62," does not inform us about the number of leaves that were extant when Emmel saw them, or are extant today.

THE AMOUNT OF LOSS SINCE 1983

The exact amount that has been lost since the codex was first seen in 1983 is unclear. A few years ago Roberty is reported to have been rather pessimistic:[43]

Roberty hopes passionately that one day another copy of *The Gospel of Judas* will turn up, because the copy as owned by the Maecenas Foundation is only 65 to 70 percent complete. "We assume that some fragments are still wandering around on the market here and there, but I am afraid that a quarter of the manuscript has been lost forever."

But Thiede's comment that Mia's fragments "evaporate for a long time" does tantalize the imagination: Does this mean that they did not evaporate forever? Henk Schutten reported that Michel van Rijn helped search for the missing fragments, and in the process made up with Roberty:[44]

But lately they settled their disagreements. Van Rijn even conducted some research for the Maecenas Foundation regarding the missing fragments of *The Gospel of Judas*, and successfully, so he said. "Roberty offered me to act as project consultant," says Van Rijn: "I was offered 50,000 pounds and a share in the foundation. My name would also be mentioned as one of the discoverers of the manuscript."

This much Roberty has confirmed:[45]

Mario Roberty confirms that Michel van Rijn did some work for the Maecenas Foundation. "Van Rijn would provide us with further information about the lost fragments of *The Gospel of Judas*. He received a payment of 50,000 pounds."

Later on, in his interview with Stacy Meichtry on February 13–14, 2006, Roberty provides more details of the damage, but also a more encouraging estimate of what has survived:[46]

You will see it's in awful shape. . . . Initial estimates, when you looked at it, were just desperate.

It was painstaking puzzle work. It will probably be going on for some time.

Each page is put under glass. It's incredibly brittle and in bad shape. I marveled myself to see how they were able to work on such material.

As to the original sequence, Roberty conceded:

Not received in original sequence, but they are confident to have the right order now. Small fragments that couldn't be precisely attributed . . .

As to page numbers, Roberty reports:

Yes it does, but just on the upper part. The whole is cut into parts, so the lower parts cannot be attributed in their page numbering to the upper parts. This has to be done following the fiber structure and also the content.

With regard to fragments, Roberty reports:

There were some souvenir hunters laying their hands on it. Partially reclaimed.

The reference to some fragments being "partially reclaimed" is intriguing, especially since others had spoken of some fragments being secondarily reunited with the whole, in which connection Van Rijn had claimed some credit. But there seems also to have been a quite recent acquisition of fragments. For Roberty, in his most recent interview, has justified a delay in the publication of the critical edition as follows:

. . . because we had a few more fragments popping up very recently. So there will be—for a full publication of the codex—there will be a delay.

Roberty provides a final encouraging report of what has been brought together: "85 percent of the main text." That is, after all, considerably better than his earlier report. Things may have turned out better than he had feared.

THE NUMBER OF PAGES IN THE TRACTATE

When one seeks to provide an estimate of the original length of the text of *The Gospel of Judas,* then the question of the number of pages in the codex that contained *The Gospel of Judas* is posed in a different way: whatever documentation one has for a leaf from that tractate suffices to indicate that the two pages of that leaf are to be included in the calculation of the original length of *The Gospel of Judas.*

Emmel identified three tractates in the codex. Since he did not thumb through all thirty leaves, looking for tractate titles and the like, there is no way of knowing whether other tractates may have been in the codex, even though not noticed by Emmel. We speak of there having been three tractates, so long as we do not know of others. Two have parallels in the Nag Hammadi Library, and so their length is known. *The (First) Apocalypse of James* (Codex V, Tractate 3, 24,10–44,10) is twenty-one pages long. *The Letter of Peter to Philip* (Codex VIII, Tractate 2, 132,10–140,27) is just over nine pages long. This makes a total of about thirty pages.

Of course the amount of text found on a given page varies, depending on the dimensions of the leaves, the amount of empty papyrus taken up in margins, the size of the scribe's lettering, the space between the lines, etc. But since the manuscript is comparable in size (Steve Emmel: "approximately 30 cm tall and 15 cm broad)"[47] to Nag Hammadi codices, the rough comparison will be useful. If the two known tractates occupied half of "up to 60" pages, that would leave sufficient room for *The Gospel of Judas* to have occupied up to thirty pages.

One may also recall Epiphanius's comment, "a short work." In his time, a book would be more the size of a canonical Gospel, so perhaps one can infer that *The Gospel of Judas* was more the size of the Gospel of Mark than the size of the larger Gospels of Matthew, Luke, and John. Of course there were much longer works, such as the Nag Hammadi tractates *Tripartite Tractate* (Codex I, Tractate 5), of 88 pages, and *Zostrianos* Codex VIII, Tractate 1), of 132 pages. But in the Nag Hammadi Library they are more the exception than the rule. But if "at least pp. 1–50 are represented by substantial fragments," there may be fewer than 30 pages from *The Gospel of Judas* that are extant in "substantial fragments," especially in view of the damage and loss that may well have occurred since Emmel saw them.

Thiede of course gives us more "information" (or speculation):[48]

The Judas document occupies fully the half of the 62 inscribed book pages, the remainder consists of two other writings.

We can surely hope that he is right, but there is no reason to assume he has such precise information.

With *The Gospel of Judas* lost for almost 1,800 years, the discovery and selling of it is a colorful story, replete with smugglers, black-market antiquities dealers, religious scholars, backstabbing partners, and greedy entrepreneurs, meeting secretly over the course of two decades across the borders of two or three continents. It is a story worthy of the myths about this most notorious disciple. But what will this lost and then found *Gospel of Judas* reveal to us? Once restored and published, will it exonerate Judas? Will it turn Christianity on its head? Let us now turn to those questions in the next chapter as I try to explain what is involved in the conserving and editing of such ancient manuscripts, and speculate with others on the meaning and significance of this remarkable discovery.

SIX

The Publication
and Significance of
The Gospel of Judas

THE BIBLIOTHÈQUE BODMER

Mario J. Roberty had mentioned in his memorandum of December 15, 2000, to Eric R. Kaufman:[1]

> The whole conservation process preferably is to be conducted in a highly reputable private institution disposing of the necessary secure facilities (e.g. the Bodmer Foundation in Celigny) by outside professionals. This should guarantee the best possible control. The exploration and evaluation of such institution will be the first task to be carried out by the Foundation.

The Bibliothèque Bodmer, in Celigny, a suburb just outside Geneva, is of course an appropriate place, the most appropriate place in Switzerland, for such a manuscript to be stored, conserved, and edited. In fact, it is where priceless third-century papyrus copies of the Gospels of Luke and John in Greek are housed ($\mathfrak{P}^{66}$ and $\mathfrak{P}^{75}$). It was created to be a repository for the many acquisitions of its founder, the distinguished

Swiss man of letters (and vice president of the International Red Cross), Martin Bodmer. A number of the manuscripts he acquired are in Coptic.[2] Years ago, a young pastor, Rodolphe Kasser, was employed to edit them. It would hence be very convenient, once he was chosen to edit *The Gospel of Judas*, for him to work on it there again, as he had in his youth. He lives within convenient commuting distance.

I can tell you about Kasser's famous Paris speech of July 1, 2004, for I was there, as I am honorary president of the International Association for Coptic Studies whose Congress was taking place. In the brief time for discussion following Kasser's presentation, I was one of the few to comment. I limited my brief remarks to the fact that the manuscript had been seen in 1983 by Steven Emmel (who had organized the Congress, and to whom I had just turned over my few hardly legible photographs of some of the pages), and that the discovery had already been announced to the scholarly world in publications as early as 1984.

Rodolphe Kasser's name provided an opportunity to Michel Van Rijn, who cannot resist an opportunity to make a humorous pun, no matter how inappropriate it may be:[3]

> Rodolphe is not to be confused with the red-nosed reindeer. This one's as brown-nosed as they come.

As if this pun is not bad enough, Van Rijn thought of the German word for cash register: "Kasse." He could not resist using it as a play on words with "Kasser":

> They await its publication (with, of course, full transcription) from Frieda's payrolled Rodolphe 'Cash' Kasse (oops, I mean Kasser). . . . Cash-&-Kasser is hoping to publish the manuscript . . .

It's only fortunate that Kasser's last name isn't "Golden"! But to think of Kasser as having a "money-bag" mentality is very inappropriate, as I know firsthand. Kasser and I worked together year after year, a couple of weeks each time, at the Coptic Museum in Cairo, reassembling the fragments of the Nag Hammadi Codices into publishable leaves. We worked seven days a week, from the time the museum opened in the morning until it closed at 2 PM. We stayed at the same hotel, the Garden City House, a cheap "pensione" run by an amicable Italian lady named Scarzella. Her establishment was frequented by archeologists and scholars to such an extent that every day she posted the list of those staying there, so that we could know who was there and visit with one another. Kasser and I thus had our very modest meals together. I never saw him making costly expenditures or showing any interest in money. He was much more the shy, scholarly recluse.

THE NATIONAL GEOGRAPHIC SOCIETY

Michel Van Rijn commented in his Web site in December 2004:[4]

> ### NATIONAL GEOGRAPHIC THOUGHT THEIR BIGGEST COMPETITORS WERE THE DISCOVERY CHANNEL . . . BUT IT'S US!
>
> . . . this weekend National Geographic will film and photograph the Gospel's fragmentary pages in a vault in Switzerland. But of what value is their "world exclusive" if they are unaware of the diggers, smugglers, art-dealers, governments and bankers alike [who] are backstabbing one other for ownership of the Gospel.

This would seem to be the first disclosure of the involvement of the National Geographic Society in the saga of *The Gospel of Judas,* though what they had in mind with their photographs was not made clear, and Van Rijn's passing comment went largely unnoticed at the time. The cloak of secrecy surrounding the discovery and publication of *The Gospel of Judas* seems to have prevailed, until it was more formally broken by me, in a presentation at the annual meeting of the Society of Biblical Literature in Philadelphia on November 20, 2005.

UTMOST SECRECY

In the memorandum sent by Mario J. Roberty to Eric R. Kaufman on December 15, 2000, item 18 specified:[5]

> It is clearly understood by all persons involved that nobody, not even Bruce and Frieda but only the Foundation, will have the right to promulgate and commercialize any knowledge regarding, concerning or deriving from the manuscripts. Moreover, for the time being and until all legal aspects are clarified, it is in the best interest of the Project to maintain utmost secrecy about its existence.

This policy of utmost secrecy has been criticized repeatedly as inappropriate in the scholarly community, but largely to no avail.

Marvin Meyer reported to us a year ago that he knows much more about what is going on regarding *The Gospel of Judas,* but has been obliged to sign a document promising not to divulge what he knows. Indeed, on October 30, 2005, in preparing my report on what I could learn about *The Gospel of Judas* to be presented on November 20, 2005, at the annual meeting of the Society of Biblical Literature in Philadelphia,[6] I asked him by e-mail if he could provide me with even minimal information about the source of his information. To quote in full his e-mailed reply: "I'm sorry—but I must say, no comment."

But then I had a stroke of good fortune. I received a phone call from Paris, from the scientific journalist Patrick Jean-Baptiste, who was writing an essay for the French monthly *Sciences et Avenir.*[7] He interviewed me by phone on November 9, 2005, after having just talked by phone the same day with Mario Roberty of the Maecenas Foundation. At my request, he e-mailed me what he had learned from Roberty, which he had kindly agreed to do. Thus he provided very up-to-date information for my presentation:

The Maecenas Foundation (Mario Roberty and Frieda Nussberger-Tchacos) had signed a very good agreement with National Geographic for the intellectual exploitation of *The Gospel of Judas.* (Actually, I do not [know] how much N[ational] G[eographic] paid, but I heard nearly a million $!!!)

The negotiations with Bruce Ferrini failed because the lawyers of this merchant from Akron, Ohio, advised him not to sign the partnership Roberty and Tchacos offered him (the first offer was of 2 millions $, the second less).

So, next year around Easter, Roberty told me, will be broadcast a documentary film about *The Gospel of Judas* and [they will] publish an article in *N[ational] G[eographic]* magazine.

Also, three books will be published by N[ational] G[eographic]. The first one: a big book with pictures of the gospel and 3 language translations (English, French, German) and commentaries by Rodolphe Kasser, Gregor Wurtz, Marvin Meyer and François Godard. The second book, more journalistic, will be written by an American producer/journalist named Harp Krosney—it will be about the story of the documents. The third book, a popularized version of the Gospel, will be written by Kasser and also a certain Bart Ehrman.

This report at the SBL convention, in a panel that had not only me but also Marvin Meyer on the platform as a panelist, created something of a sensation, as one might well imagine. It was the first clarification of what necessitates Meyer's silence.

Jean-Baptiste was thus the first to publish the specifics of the project of the National Geographic Society as follows:[8]

> Today, no longer does anyone have access to this text. An ad hoc foundation, the Maecenas Foundation based in Basel, Switzerland, owns it and has just negotiated a wonderful contract of exclusivity with the National Geographic Society. In theory, nothing is to leak out before Easter 2006, date of the diffusion of a grand documentary film and of the publication of three books. As to the announcement of the Maecenas Foundation, according to which the codex will then be restored to the Egyptians, this is not able to make one forget that at the beginning it was quite simply stolen, then exported illegally . . .

He also published the names of those involved, as follows:[9]

> "This codex will be published completely translated in English, German, and French, with all the photographic material, in the form of a handsome book destined for specialists," rejoices Mario Roberty, the director of the Maecenas Foundation for Ancient Art, Basel, who retains the Gospel. "This work will be co-signed by the Professor Rodolphe Kasser, to whom we have confided the manuscript in 2002, as well as the Professors Gregor Wurst, François Godard and Marvin Meyer."

The volume soon to appear with the translation apparently will not include the Coptic. This is a decisive difference! Omitting the Coptic would, in effect, maintain the monopoly until Roberty saw fit to publish the Coptic, since only then could others translate it and publish it on their own. And of course a preliminary translation could be published the week after Easter, which seems to be required by the contract with the National Geographic Society, without actually having finished the placement of fragments and the other dimensions necessary for a definitive *editio princeps*.

STEVE EMMEL TO THE RESCUE

I inquired of Steve Emmel whether what I was planning to say in this book about his interest in Gnosticism, and his resultant interest in the Nag Hammadi Codices and the Coptic language, was all correct. To my surprise, in his reply (from Cairo, Egypt, where he has been studying Shenoute manuscripts) he casually, almost sheepishly, added:

> By the way, I want to tell you that I—with some reluctance—just yesterday agreed to join the National Geographic Society's "Codex Project Advisory Panel," which means that I have signed an agreement not to reveal information that N[ational] G[eographic] S[ociety] has given me confidentially. Believe it or not, up until now this information has not (repeat: has not) included knowledge of the contents of *The Gospel of Judas*. Frankly, I would rather not have any privileged access to that, and I am going to try to avoid having any knowledge of it until my agreement with N[ational] G[eographic] S[ociety] absolutely requires it (for instance, if they want my opinion on it at some point prior to its publication). Furthermore, nothing of what I have learned only through my association with N[ational] G[eographic] S[ociety] (which goes

back to fall 2004 or a little earlier) is of any great interest, in my humble opinion, but I am not a member of the
innermost circle. . . .

What I want to tell you is this: I have joined the
N[ational] G[eographic] S[ociety] advisory panel and
signed their confidentiality agreement as a way—I sin-
cerely hope!—of getting into a position to ensure that the
Coptic text of *The Gospel of Judas* will be made publicly
accessible as soon as possible, in any case no later than
the publication of the first "authorized" translation of it.
I have been working on this angle for some time now and
think that I have now secured adequate assurances from
N[ational] G[eographic] S[ociety]. In return, and to have
the best hope of holding them to their word, I had to agree
to join the gang. D-Day is still set for around Easter this
year, so stay tuned. If things go wrong, I will make at least
some kind of a stink. . . .

I have cautioned N[ational] G[eographic] S[ociety]
against sensationalism, and I do think that the principals
there want to avoid the stupid kind of sensationalism
that the press loves so much. But there are some people
involved in the project who do not seem to understand
much of anything except stupid sensationalism, and so I
can certainly not guarantee that the publication of the text
and translation will not be accompanied by some phoney
hoopla. In any case, surely the media will try to sensation-
alize it just because of the title *"The Gospel of Judas."*
For my own part, I will continue to try to emphasize the
genuine scientific interest of this codex (and every other
ancient manuscript), which in a perfect world would be
(intellectually speaking) sensational enough.

I'm simply delighted that Steve has become a member of
the National Geographic Society's "Codex Project Advisory

Panel," and thus is an insider as to what is going on. It gives me hope that things will be done right. Obviously he will not succeed in delaying the publication of the translation until the Coptic transcription can also be published, since the translation is due out about now, and Roberty reports that fragments are still being placed and thus the conservation has not been completed, much less the *editio princeps* with the Coptic transcription. But as Emmel brought the publication of the Nag Hammadi Codices almost single-handedly to a successful completion, after the Technical Subcommittee of UNESCO's International Committee for the Nag Hammadi Codices had ceased to function, I know firsthand that no one would be a better addition to the team at this eleventh hour.

One may recall how Emmel recommended in his memorandum of June 1, 1983, the conservation of the newly discovered Coptic Gnostic codex:

> The leaves and fragments of the codex will need to be conserved between panes of glass. I would recommend conservation measures patterned after those used to restore and conserve the Nag Hammadi Codices (see my article, "The Nag Hammadi Codices Editing Project: A Final Report," American Research Center in Egypt, Inc., *Newsletter* 104 [1978] 10–32). Despite the breakage that has already occurred, and that which will inevitably occur between now and the proper conservation of the manuscript, I estimate that it would require about a month to reassemble the fragments of the manuscript and to arrange the reassembled leaves between panes of glass.

As I read this, I could almost see Steve drooling at the mouth, he was so eager to get his hands on the material and conserve it properly before more damage was done to it. That did not happen in 1983. But now, twenty-three years later, Herr Prof. Dr.

Emmel may have the chance he has been waiting for so very long. I see a light at the end of the tunnel!

It should be pointed out that this final verification of the accurate placements of fragments on the leaves, indeed the completion of the reassembling of a very fragmentary papyrus codex, is precisely one of Emmel's specialties. As he mentioned in the paragraph just quoted from his memorandum, he did write the "Final Report" on "The Nag Hammadi Codices Editing Project." The much more detailed itemization of all he did to wrap up that project to its successful conclusion is in the final volume of *The Facsimile Edition of the Nag Hammadi Codices*, somewhat innocently entitled *Introduction*. There, after introductory chapters I wrote, there is an extensive section of *corrigenda* composed for all intents and purposes by Steve. All thirteen Nag Hammadi Codices have been published in facsimile volumes as rapidly as we could, so as to break the monopoly on this discovery and make it available to everyone. But that meant that there were inevitably slight improvements and additions that could be added to those volumes, especially in the placement of fragments.

Let's take, for example, an instance of what we called an "island" placement, where a fragment does not actually touch the fragmentary leaf to which it belongs, but can be identified by the postulated flow of the lettering of the text. All too often what was involved was a small fragment with only a single letter legible on it. Who cares if it was placed a centimeter out of its correct position? Well, anyone trying to edit that text cares! Where it is shown in the volume of *The Facsimile Edition* that has already appeared has been a pain for everyone working on the text. What is missing in the line on which it occurs seems to be easily and convincingly reconstructed, except for one detail: that letter on the little fragment does not fit in the otherwise convincing reconstruction of that line! If only we didn't have

that letter to cope with—but now we don't, thanks to the little note in the *corrigenda* that it is to be raised (or lowered) a
centimeter. That means it is no longer in that line, but in the
line just above (or below). That may sound to you like a circu-
lar argument: if you don't like it where it is, just get rid of it!
But Steve would rather die than commit such a sin! Rather, he
had traced the horizontal fiber pattern on the body of that leaf
across the gap and onto the small fragment, and had seen that
the fiber pattern did not fit. But by raising (or lowering) the fragment precisely one centimeter, the horizontal fiber pattern does
work! So that is why he changed the position in the *corrigenda*.
And then, after the prose description of hundreds of such minor
improvements, there are photographs of just the relevant lines
with the fragment in its correct position. Steve had opened the
sealed Plexiglas container where that leaf had been conserved,
loosened with a drop of water the sliver of transparent tape holding down that fragment (not Scotch tape, but special tape manu-
factured just for this purpose), and moved the fragment precisely
one centimeter up (or down). Then, with a sliver of transparent
tape, he reattached it to the lower pane of Plexiglas and resealed
the two panes together. And that is how you will find it if you
visit the Coptic Museum today!

This is what still needs doing at the Bibliothèque Bodmer
near Geneva, before Roberty considers the conservation task
finally achieved, which means before Kasser publishes the final
transcription and translation in the *editio princeps*. So let me
draw this to the attention of Roberty, who has, I naively hope,
read the book thus far: now is the moment to prick up your ears
and see what still needs to be done to implement your general-
izing comment that, since "it was painstaking puzzle work,"
"it will probably be going on for some time," quite apart from
"a few more fragments popping up very recently" that you give
as the reason that "there will be a delay."

HOW A PAPYRUS CONSERVATION LAB FUNCTIONS

Of course I have not been given access to the conservation laboratory, presumably in the Bibliothèque Bodmer near Geneva, where the actual work of reassembling the fragmentary leaves of the codex containing *The Gospel of Judas* has actually been taking place. But I once organized such a lab, in which both Kasser and Emmel worked! As permanent secretary of the International Committee for the Nag Hammadi Codices, I enlisted the Technical Sub-Committee to work for several years, a week or so at a time, in the Coptic Museum in Cairo, doing precisely this same kind of work of placing fragments on tattered papyrus leaves and thus preparing the codices for photography and publication. As a result, I know firsthand what has to be done. I even know how Kasser works in such a situation, since he and I worked side-by-side in the Coptic Museum, after I enlisted him as a member of the Technical Sub-Committee. So I can with some justification imagine what is going on, I think with more reliability than any outsider could.

Kasser proved to be a very conscientious, laborious, punctilious, scrupulous, meticulous, exacting technical worker with papyrus, from the time the museum opened in the morning until it closed in the afternoon. There is no doubt that he knows from personal experience how to do the work that needs to be done in conserving the codex that contains *The Gospel of Judas*. But he also has the responsibility for transcribing, translating, and publishing the text in the *editio princeps*, with its introduction, notes, and indices of Coptic words, Greek loan words, and proper names. He really does not have time to do the actual physical placement of fragments as well!

The Bibliothèque Bodmer did not have on its staff, the last time I visited it, a papyrus conservator. Presumably Kasser has enlisted people to do this work for him. How many, how regularly, with how much experience behind them? They must have had employment prior to this—did they get a leave of absence, or are they moonlighting? Do they have to come and go, or are they working full-time on this project? How long have they been at it? How many hours a day? At the Coptic Museum, we wanted to work more hours per day than the museum was open, so they finally broke down and gave me a key to the room where we worked, so that we could work after hours as long as we wanted. Do the conservators have unlimited access to their laboratory, or are their hours restricted? How are they reassembling the leaves from fragments, and establishing the sequence of the leaves?

Since I worked with Kasser in Cairo doing this same kind of task, I know the procedure that he must be implementing there.

First of all, there are (at least) three different tractates in the codex. The first task may be to sort the fragments, to determine to which tractate each fragment belongs. This could be relatively easy, since there are duplicates of two of the tractates in the Nag Hammadi Codices. Fortunately, the critical editions of the Nag Hammadi Codices include indices. One could readily look up in these indices any words that are legible on the fragments of the new codex, and determine if the fragment in question belongs to one or the other of these two previously known tractates. But in actual practice it is not all that simple. For the Coptic translations in the new codex are apparently different translations from those used in the Nag Hammadi Codices, or the Greek from which they were translated differs, or both. As a result, a fragment may belong to one of those tractates but not be identifiable as such, because it involves a slight variation in wording. It is hence not certain that every fragment that cannot be placed in this way in one of the two previously known tractates belongs, by the process of elimination, to *The Gospel of Judas*.

The easiest fragment placements are of course those that occur when one fragment has the letters of part of a word and another fragment (or fragmentary leaf) has the other letters of that same word, and the two fit together nicely, as in a jigsaw puzzle. But one is not usually so lucky! There are many island placements, where a fragment does not actually touch the fragmentary leaf to which it belongs, but can be identified by the postulated flow of the lettering of the text. But this involves a higher degree of uncertainty.

Of course even the most "certain" placement must be verified by the continuity of fibers from one to the other. The fiber patterns serve as the "fingerprints" of papyrus, since no two sheets of papyrus have exactly the same pattern of papyrus strips. This flow of fibers, which are horizontal on one side and vertical on the other, confirms that the placement of a fragment is correct. Sometimes an identification can be made on the basis of the fibers, even though there is no recognizable continuity of lettering, and even if the two fragments do not actually touch and fit into each other's edge.

When a fragment is thus "placed," it is taken out of the mass of unidentified fragments and put together with the leaf or other fragment with which it belongs, together between panes of glass in their correct positioning in relation to each other, awaiting hopefully further fragments being placed on that same leaf. Thus bit by bit a leaf grows, sometimes beginning quite humbly with one medium-sized fragment, or only with a couple of small fragments that belong together, into, one hopes, a much fuller leaf. But even if it remains so minimal, it is still evidence of a leaf in the original codex, deserving to be counted if one seeks to determine the number of leaves that originally made up the codex, even if, for all practical purposes, that leaf is lost.

Only when all the conservation that is possible has taken place is one really in a position to count how many panes of glass with the remains of a *leaf* there are, in distinction from panes of glass containing only unidentified *fragments*.

The comments of Roberty in the interview of February 13–14, 2006, are hence very understandable:

> It was painstaking puzzle work. It will probably be going on for some time.

> . . . because we had a few more fragments popping up very recently. So there will be—for a full publication of the codex—there will be a delay.

Publication the week after Easter, April 17–21, just two months after admitting that fragment placement "will probably be going on for some time," "a delay"? Of course, Kasser knew how much time such work takes when he promised in his speech of July 1, 2004, to publish the *editio princeps* by the end of 2005, a deadline that no one expected him to meet. But then the National Geographic Society required a deadline of the week after Easter (April 16, 2006), to profit most from Easter always being the occasion for a Christian focus in the news magazines, not to mention the release of the film version of *The Da Vinci Code* (May 17, 2006). The team was enlarged, and focus must have been shifted away from a complete *editio princeps* that would include the Coptic text as well as the translation(s), to what may only be a preliminary popularizing translation, no matter what assurances Emmel thinks he has received. Roberty has already provided the excuse for not meeting the promised deadlines with a definitive work. Kasser could have provided these explanations from the very beginning, but no doubt had to agree to meet a 2005 deadline in order to get the assignment for himself. Once he had the assignment and the work was well underway, one deadline extension after the other would be understandable, and, for some of us, predictable.

THE SIGNIFICANCE OF *THE GOSPEL OF JUDAS*

So what will be the significance of *The Gospel of Judas*? In his interview by the German news magazine *FOCUS* Steve Emmel makes some sound speculations:[10]

EMMEL: Naturally the text awakens, because of its pretended author, the interest on the most varied sides. How interesting it will ultimately be, we do not yet know. Certainly it was not written by Judas Iscariot himself (*laughs*) . . .

FOCUS: It has to do with a pseudepigraph . . .

EMMEL: . . . Exactly, a genre that contains fictional ascriptions to apostolic authors. Decisive is whether the text provides a new perspective on the early history of Christianity. Up until now, one cannot speak of that. The people who previously owned the codex always thought only about money. Also the current owners are out for sensation. I still doubt though that the text proves to be so terribly exciting. There are hundreds of unpublished Coptic manuscripts, only none have such sensational a title.

FOCUS: Is the delay in publication a scandal?

EMMEL: . . . at least I would not work that way. I would have produced a provisional edition. Normally experts exchange texts one with another. Here it is apparently the goal to stay covered so that once it appears everyone will immediately buy the book. One understands: He who has access to an especially interesting text will perhaps always want to win something from it: money, fame, honor, or whatever.

FOCUS: For a long time there are attempts to define in a new way the relation of heresy and orthodoxy, in early

Christianity, for example in the sense that the Gnostic "heresy" presented perhaps the original part of Christianity. Will *The Gospel of Judas* play a roll here?

EMMEL: There are people who believe that, or want to believe it. The topic could become exciting—if the new text were to prove once for all that in the beginning Christianity was completely different. For 2000 years the church has invested a great deal in the orthodox form of its history. It uses a historical myth to support faith. Scholars have said for a long time that the history must have taken place differently. But what really happened back then is debated. Also the Gospels of the Bible were probably not written by eyewitnesses. Most probably we will never learn who Jesus was or whether there ever was such a person. The new material no doubt shows only, still another time, that early Christianity is to be seen very diversely. Much is unclear as to what counted then as genuine, heretical or orthodox.

FOCUS: What religious thought lurks behind *The Gospel of Judas*?

EMMEL: The most interesting thing will be whether a theologically thought-out reason for the betrayal of Judas is named. We already know sources according to which Judas is a hero in a certain sense, since without him the Christian salvation history could not have taken its course.

FOCUS: A conscious blasphemy is excluded?

EMMEL: Not necessarily. The authors of these texts were partly very smart people who found the simple faith a bit laughable. It can be that it had to do with putting orthodox concepts intentionally on their head. That belongs to the spirit of the second century, in which the doctrine of Gnosticism reached its peak.

There has been much speculation on what the discovery of *The Gospel of Judas* would mean for the Roman Catholic Church. The Swiss reporter Ralph Pöhner writes:[11]

> The name alone—*Gospel of Judas*!—may inflame theses of conspiracy and provoke speculation as to whether the Pope now needs to tremble and the Vatican is shaken in its foundations.

But he has to concede that this is hardly probable:[12]

> What the text really signifies theologically is another question. "I doubt," says Charles W. Hedrick, "that the leaders of organized Christianity will waste a second thought on it, once the excitement about its discovery has once passed."

Thiede has also picked up on this potential sensation:[13]

> Internet authors, in the style of Dan Brown's super-seller critical of Rome, *The Da Vinci Code*, have long since fabricated stories about the "unheard of shock waves" of the text, which will soon "shake" the Catholic Church "in its foundations." The public prepares itself to be able possibly to buy the original text of an ancient "Anti-Bible," which presents the pre-Easter events in the year of Jesus' death (or, if one prefers, only in early church history) in a completely different light from what the orthodox presentations have to offer.

Yet it is not simply a matter of scholars being able to choose whichever one prefers, "pre-Easter events in the year of Jesus' death" or something "in early church history." They do not have the choice between what their research convinces them is historically accurate and what is just sensational. *The Gospel of Judas* is a second-century apocryphal Gospel that in all probability tells us about the Cainite Gnostics of the mid-second century, not about what happened in AD 30!

Even Henk Schutten publishes a newspaper report in *Het Parool* entitled "Is there a copy in the Vatican," for which he interviewed Roberty:

> Roberty does not rule out at all that the Vatican owns a copy of their own all this time, securely locked away. "In those days the Church decided for political reasons to include the Gospels of Luke, Mark, Matthew and John in the Bible. The other gospels were banned. It is highly logical that the Catholic Church would have kept a copy of the forbidden gospels. Sadly, the Vatican does not want to clarify further. Their policy has been the same for years: "No further comment."

In the early centuries, there was no such thing as the Vatican, much less a Vatican library. But even if the Church had had a copy, which is of course pure speculation, would they have retained it through all the centuries—when the capital of the Roman Empire moved to Constantinople, when Rome was captured by the Goths, when the Vatican moved to Avignon, France, when the old basilica was replaced by the present cathedral? It is very, very, unlikely that a copy is safely hidden away in the Vatican archives, and if it were, it would be highly unlikely that anyone on the staff at the Vatican knows that it is. Such speculation is simply invented to heighten the sensationalism, while designed to discredit the Roman Catholic Church.

Stephen C. Carlson tried to put this to rest once for all, but apparently without success:[14]

The Australian *Daily Telegraph* now has an article about it: "Controversial gospel to be translated" (Mar. 30, 2005). The news article relies heavily on a person from a certain Maecenas Foundation in Basel, Switzerland, which seems to be involved in exploiting this document. . . .

Another aspect of the news article is no news: "'We do not want to reveal the exceptional side of what we have,' Mr. Roberty said,"—except that "the Judas Iscariot text called into question some of the political principles of Christian doctrine."

Nevertheless, that did not prevent the article having its *Da Vinci Code* moment:

The Roman Catholic Church limited the recognized gospels to the four in AD 325, under the guidance of the first Christian Roman emperor, Constantine.

Thirty other texts—some of which have been uncovered—were sidelined because "they were difficult to reconcile with what Constantine wanted as a political doctrine," according to Mr. Roberty.

Not this canard again. The canonization of the New Testament was a long process that began well before Constantine and ended decisively decades after him. . . .

Given how Mr. Roberty is quoted, it is not clear whether he is fully responsible for this historical nonsense . . .

A newspaper in Turin, Italy, *La Stampa*, reported on January 11, 2006, that some sources said the apocryphal manuscript would lead to a favorable reevaluation of Judas. This was picked up January 12, 2006, by the London *Times*, in an article written by Richard Owen according to the byline, with the headline "Judas the Misunderstood" and the subtitle "Vatican moves to clear reviled disciple's name." It says of Monsignor Walter

Brandmüller, president of the Pontifical Committee for Historical Science, that he is leading a campaign "aimed at persuading believers to look kindly at a man reviled for 2,000 years." Then this article was followed the next day, January 13, 2006, by an article in the London *Times*, written by Ben MacIntyre according to the byline, entitled "Blamed, framed or defamed. Three good reasons to free the Judas One." This essay is clearly a spoof, formulated as Judas's defense attorney's final appeal to the jury to acquit him. There is a similar article the same day, January 13, 2006, in the London *Guardian*, written by John Crace according to the byline, entitled "Judas Iscariot: his life and good works":

> Reports emanating from the Vatican suggest that the Catholic Church may be about to rehabilitate the reputation of Judas, the apostle commonly held to have betrayed Jesus. Scholars now suggest that, in fact, Judas was merely "fulfilling his part in God's plan." Below, we pre-empt the possible rewriting of the gospel.

Thereupon follows a rewriting of the canonical story, which is ridiculous, or infuriating, or both, only to conclude:

> Jesus blessed him. "I forgive you now, but it will take everyone else 2,000 years." And so it came to pass.

This was followed up on January 16, 2006, in the *Toronto Star*, written by Rosie DiManno according to the byline, entitled "Judas reborn: Are we ready to rethink the fink?" It retraces the same steps as the other newspaper articles of the preceding days, only to end: "It's scheduled for publication at Easter. Nice timing."

But Monsignor Brandmüller told the Catholic news agency of Rome, ZENIT: "I have not talked with *The Times*. I can't imagine where this idea came from." "This news has no foundation." He went on to explain:

> In regard to the manuscript, it must be emphasized that the apocryphal gospels belong in the main to a special literary genre, a sort of religious novel that cannot be considered as a documentary source for the historical figure of Judas.

When it was suggested that the rehabilitation of Judas would favor the dialogue with Jews, Monsignor Brandmüller replied:

> The dialogue between the Holy See and the Jews continues profitably on other bases, as Benedict XVI mentioned in his visit to the Synagogue of Cologne, in the summer of 2005 during World Youth Day, and as he stressed last Monday in his meeting with the chief rabbi of Rome.

In an interview late in January 2006 with Stacy Meichtry, the Vatican correspondent of the Religious News Service, Monsignor Brandmüller is even more explicit:

> This gospel is apocryphal—a kind of historical fiction. Religiously and theologically it is of no interest. But it helps to illustrate the literary scene of ancient Christianity . . . for thought that is non-religious and non-theological. It is a literary work, not a religious or theological text. With all probability, the author knew that. He knew what he was writing.
>
>   There is no campaign, no movement to rehabilitate the traitor of Jesus. The reports are absolutely false. . . . One has to admit that the figure of Judas has always been a mystery. As a result he has stirred much speculation and attempts to interpret his betrayal. But an accepted expla-

nation does not exist. The mystery remains. He remains a figure on the margins.

We welcome the publication of a critical edition like we welcome the study of any text of ancient literature.

A fan club, a group, never existed. Some one (an individual) probably went to work writing a novel on Judas.

Much could depend on the critical study of the text itself. Some small finding could emerge, but I don't believe so. It is a product of religious fantasy. Usually these apocryphal gospels originate from a desire to know details beyond that which we read in the gospels.

Thus the Roman Catholic Church has maintained its calm, reaffirming its traditional position, and refusing to be drawn into a discussion one way or the other that could only serve the sensationalists.

Actually, this dimension of the story had already been anticipated, if you will, even prior to *The Gospel of Judas* becoming the sensation that it now threatens to become. A novel was published in 2000, entitled, of all things, *The Gospel of Judas: A Novel.* A priest in Rome, Father Leo Newman, receives fragments of a first century scroll (of course) found near the Dead Sea (of course), which he is to decipher. It is an account of Jesus's life apparently written by Judas even before the canonical Gospels, explaining that Jesus did not rise from the dead. Father Leo realizes it could blow apart the foundation of Christianity and of his own life as a believing priest. So when he is called upon to validate and interpret the fragments, everything comes apart.

This book, apparently written without knowledge of the ancient Coptic papyrus manuscript of *The Gospel of Judas,* does in substance what some would expect (want?) the real *Gospel of Judas* to effect. But amazon.com lists one hundred new and used copies available from $0.49.

Pöhner cannot help concluding his story on his own secu-
lar note:[15]

A fictional story. In our unchristian time the text appears
as a weighty historical document, though its religious
power will have limits. Yet perhaps it can arouse our fantasy: What, if the view of that Judas priest had prevailed?
What significance would then loyalty have for us, what
would betrayal be? What was the lie?

Of course the publication of the translation of *The Gospel of
Judas* will in effect end this tempest in a teapot, just as the publication of the long-withheld parts of the Dead Sea Scrolls and
the Nag Hammadi Codices did.

In the case of the Dead Sea Scrolls, a sensational effort was
undertaken to use the Scrolls to discredit the Roman Catholic
Church. Robert W. Eisenman, a Jewish scholar at Long Beach
State University, had launched the theory that the unpublished fragments were being withheld by the Roman Catholic
Church, lest their contents completely disprove the validity of
Christianity. He claimed that the founder of the community
that produced the Dead Sea Scrolls was none other than Jesus's
brother James! In this case James, and presumably his brother Jesus, would, just as the Teacher of Righteousness in the Dead
Sea Scrolls (whom Eisenman identified as James), advocate very
strict adherence to Judaism. This would mean that Paul's
departure from Judaism, and the church of today following
Paul's lead, is illegitimate! But this theory breaks down for a
series of very solid scholarly reasons.[16] As a result, Eisenman
did not have an academic following. But he was somehow
able to secure, out of Israel, a copy of the monopolized photographs of the unpublished fragments of the Dead Sea Scrolls.
Then he enlisted my aid, since he knew of me as a monopo-
ly-breaker in the case of the Nag Hammadi Codices, to help

him get them published. So we worked together as odd bedfel-
lows, he to prove his sensationalist theory, me to disprove it.[17]
Now that the fragments in question have been available for
over a decade, Eisenman's sensationalistic theory has simply
disappeared from the media. The Dead Sea Scrolls, which are
of great significance to scholars in the field, have been left to
them, Jewish and Christian scholars alike, to be studied carefully and soberly, free of that kind of sensationalism.

In the case of the Nag Hammadi Codices, the sensationalist
was Jean Doresse, a French graduate student who made his reputation by being the first to publicize the material in Cairo.[18]
He arranged an interview with the French-language newspaper
of Cairo, which published his sensational report:[19]

> According to the specialists consulted, it has to do with
> one of the most extraordinary discoveries preserved until
> now by the soil of Egypt, surpassing in scientific inter-
> est such spectacular discoveries as the tomb of Tut-Ankh-
> Amon.

Here again, once the Nag Hammadi Codices were published
and fully available to the public,[20] the sensationalism in the
news media disappeared and serious scholarship took over.
Of course the Nag Hammadi Codices are of great importance
for reconstructing early Christian history. But sensationalism
only serves to discredit discoveries of such importance as the
Dead Sea Scrolls and the Nag Hammadi Codices.

It will no doubt be the same in the case of *The Gospel of
Judas*. Once it becomes available, one will find that it does not
shed light on what happened during Jesus's trip to Jerusalem
(which is what the sensationalists imply), but rather will shed
light on a second-century Gnostic sect. This will be important
for scholars, but not for the sensationalists. But by then the
Maecenas Foundation will, no doubt, as the memorandum of

December 15, 2000, stipulated, have achieved its first objective:

> The promoters of the Project have incurred and will incur substantial expenses of money and time in order to realize the Project. It is a clear understanding that they shall be fully compensated and shall make a decent profit.

They can then turn *The Gospel of Judas* over to the scholarly community, to achieve the other objective stated there:

> On the other hand, it is understood that this Project leads into a dimension far beyond a commercial transaction. The manuscripts involved being of potential importance to a major part of mankind imposes an approach substantially different to an ordinary business transaction.

So let us close on that happy note!

Notes

CHAPTER ONE: THE JUDAS OF THE NEW TESTAMENT

1. *The Critical Edition of Q: Synopsis Including the Gospels of Matthew and Luke, Mark and Thomas with English, German, and French Translations of Q and Thomas,* eds. James M. Robinson, Paul Hoffmann, and John S. Kloppenborg (Minneapolis: Fortress, and Leuven: Peeters, 2000).

2. William Klassen, *Judas: Betrayer or Friend of Jesus?* (Minneapolis: Fortress, 1996).

3. Claire Clivaz, "Douze noms pour une main: nouveaux regards sur Judas à partir de Lc 22.21–22," *New Testament Studies* 48 (2002): 400–416.

CHAPTER TWO: THE HISTORICAL JUDAS

1. Origen, *Against Celsus,* 2.9, cited by William Klassen, *Judas: Betrayer or Friend?* (Minneapolis: Fortress, 1996), 138.

2. R. S. Anderson, *The Gospel according to Judas* (Colorado Springs: Helmers & Howard, 1991).

3. Hans-Josef Klauck, *Jesus: Ein Jünger des Herrn,* Quaestiones Disputatae 111 (Freiburg: Herder, 1987).

4. Klassen, *Judas.*

5. Kim Paffenroth, *Judas: Images of the Lost Disciple* (Louisville: Westminster John Knox, 2002).

6. Klassen, *Judas,* 48.

7. *A Greek-English Lexicon of the New Testament and Other Early Christian Literature,* a translation and adaptation of the fourth revised and augmented edition of Walter Bauer's *Griechisch-Deutsches Wörterbuch zu den Schriften des Neuen Testaments und der übringen urchristlichen Literatur,* by William F. Arndt and F. Wilburg Gingrich, second edition revised and augmented by F. Wilbur Gingrich and Frederick W. Danker, from Bauer's fifth edition (Chicago and London: The University of Chicago Press, 1958).

8. Klassen, *Judas,* 74.

9. The quotation is in fact from Zech. 11:12–13.

10. Klassen, *Judas.*

CHAPTER THREE: THE GNOSTIC JUDAS

1. Irenaeus, *Refutation of All Heresies*, 1.31.1.

2. Epiphanius, *Panarion*, 37.3.4–5; 6.1–2; 38.1.5.

3. Henri-Charles Puech, revised after his death by Beate Blatz, in *New Testament Apocrypha*, revised edition, ed. Wilhelm Schneemelcher, English translation ed. R. McL. Wilson, 1: *Gospels and Related Writings* (Cambridge, England: James Clarke & Co; Louisville, Ky.: Westminster/John Knox, 1991), 386–87.

4. *The Testimony of Truth*, Nag Hammadi Codex IX, Tractate 3, 45,23–48,15.

5. James M. Robinson, as Permanent Secretary of the International Committee for the Nag Hammadi Codices nominated by UNESCO and appointed by the Arab Republic of Egypt, *The Facsimile Edition of the Nag Hammadi Codices*, twelve volumes, 1972–84.

6. See my detailed analysis in *The Facsimile Edition of the Nag Hammadi Codices: Introduction* (Leiden: E. J. Brill, 1984).

7. Ralph Pöhner, "Judas der Held," *FACTS: Das Schweizer Nachrichtenmagazin* (January 6, 2005): 76–79.

8. They are reprinted in James M. Robinson, *The Sayings Gospel Q: Collected Essays*, ed. Christoph Heil and Joseph Verheyden, BETL 189 (Leuven: University Press and Uitgeverij Peeters, 2005), 711–883.

9. See my "Evaluations." Q *12:49–59: Children against Parents—Judging the Time—Settling out of Court*, Documenta Q: Reconstructions of Q Through Two Centuries of Gospel Reserarch Excerpted, Sorted, and Evaluated (Leuven: Peeters, 1997).

10. *The Fifth Gospel: The Gospel of Thomas Comes of Age*, by Steven J. Patterson and James M. Robinson, with a New English Translation by Hans-Gebhard Bethge et al. (Harrisburg, Pa.: Trinity Press International, 1998).

11. The Nag Hammadi Library in English, translated by members of the Coptic Gnostic Library Project of the Institute for Antiquity and Christianity, James M. Robinson, Director and General Editor, James M. Robinson, Managing Editor Marvin W. Meyer (Leiden: E. J. Brill, 1977, paperback edition 1984; San Francisco: Harper & Row, 1977, paperback edition 1981).

12. The *Gospel of Philip*, Nag Hammadi Codex II, Tractate 3, 73,8–19.

13. The *Gospel of the Egyptians*, Nag Hammadi Codex III, Tractate 2, 40,12–13. A second, more fragmentary copy is in Codex IV, Tractate 2.

14. The *Gospel of the Egyptians*, Nag Hammadi Codex III, Tractate 2, 69,18–20.

15. The *Gospel of the Egyptians*, Nag Hammadi Codex III, Tractate 2, 69,6–17.

16. The *Gospel of Truth*, Nag Hammadi Codex I, Tractate 3, 16,31–34.

17. A. J. Droge and J. D. Tabor, *A Noble Death: Suicide and Martyrdom among Christians and Jews in Antiquity* (San Francisco: HarperSanFrancisco, 1992), cited by Klassen, *Judas*, 168 and 175.

18. William Klassen, *Judas: Betrayer or Friend of Jesus?* (Minneapolis: Fortress, 1996), 47, quoting Augustine, *City of God*, 1.17 and *Sermon* 352.3.8 (*Patrologia Latina*, 39:1559–63).

19. The translation, by Morton S. Enslin, "How the Story Grew: Judas in Fact and Fiction," in *Festschrift in Honor of F. W. Gingrich*, ed. E. H. Barth and R. Cocroft (Leiden: Brill, 1972), is quoted by Klassen, *Judas*, 173.

20. Quoted by Klassen, *Judas*, 7.

21. Klassen, *Judas*, 18–20.

22. Roger Thiede, "Das JUDAS-Evangelium," *FOCUS* 13, 2005, 116.

23. Thiede, "Das JUDAS-Evangelium," 116.

24. English translation by M. E. Heine (London: Hutchinson, 1977).

25. Michael Dickinson, *The Lost Testament of Judas Iscariot* (Dingle, Brandon, 1994).

26. Ernest Sutherland Bates, *The Gospel of Judas* (London: William Heinemann, 1929). It had been published already in 1928 in the United States under the title *The Friend of Jesus* (New York: Simon & Schuster, 1928). But *The Gospel of Judas* was Bates's original title.

27. Hugh S. Pyper, "Modern Gospels of Judas: Canon and Betrayal," *Literature & Theology* 15 (2001): 111–22.

CHAPTER FOUR: *THE GOSPEL OF JUDAS* SURFACES IN GENEVA

1. Roger Thiede, "Das JUDAS-Evangelium," 114.

2. Ralph Pöhner, "Judas der Held," *FACTS: Das Schweitzer Nachrichtenmagazin* (January 6, 2005): 76–79.

3. Thiede, "Das JUDAS-Geheimnis," *FOCUS* 13 (2005): 107–16.

4. Malcolm Macalister Hall, "The Gospel Truth," *The Sunday Review: The Independent on Sunday* (June 5, 2005): 24–26, 28, 31.

5. Henk Schutten, "The hunt for the Gospel of Judas," in the Dutch newspaper *Het Parool*, translated by Michel van Rijn on his Web site, http:www.michelvanrijn.nl/artnews/parool-trans1.htm (February 16, 2006), available also at http://www.tertullian.org/rpearse/manuscripts/gospel_of_judas/ (February 16, 2006), misrepresented the involvement of SMU:

> Emmel, a leading American coptologist and the German papyrologist Ludwig Koenen was [sic!] sent from Dallas to Geneva by the Southern Methodist University to have a look at manuscripts that were offered for sale by shadowy merchants.
>
> Similarly Ralph Pöhner, "Judas, der Held," *FACTS*, January 6, 2005, 76–79: 78: The Southern Methodist University in Dallas showed interest, in May 1983 it sent Koenen with the coptologist Stephen Emmel to Geneva.

6. Hans Jonas, *The Gnostic Religion* (Boston: Beacon Press, 1958, 1963, 1991, 2001).

7. Stephen Emmel, "The Nag Hammadi Codices Editing Project: A Final Report," American Research Center in Egypt, *Newsletter* 104 (1978): 10–32.

8. "Ein anderes Frühchristentum?," an interview with Stephen Emmel conducted by Roger Thiede, published in *FOCUS* 13 (2005): 118–19: 118.

9. Robert Macalister Hall, "The Gospel Truth," in *The Independent on Sunday*, June 5, 2005, 24–31: 26.

10. Henk Schutten, "The hunt for the Gospel of Judas."

11. In the interview with Thiede, "Ein anderes Frühchristentum?," 118.

12. Quoted by Pöhner, "Judas, der Held," 78.

13. The existence of this work in the codex had already been discovered by Ludwig Koenen, on the basis of a few sample photographs that the sellers had sent him, when they first offered to show him this material, and which Koenen had shared with Gerald M. Brown of the University of Illinois at Champaign-Urbana in order to have the barely legible bits of text transcribed and translated.

14. For more details, see the paper I presented at the annual conference of the Society of Biblical Literature in Philadelphia on November 20, 2005, "From The Nag Hammadi Codices to *The Gospel of Mary* and *The Gospel of Judas*," published as Occasional Paper 48 by the Institute for Antiquity and Christianity, Claremont Graduate University, Claremont, Calif., 2006.

15. Listed in my Foreword to the reprint of W. E. Crum, *A Coptic Dictionary* (Eugene, Ore.: Wipf and Stock Publishers, 2005). It is on seven unnumbered pages prior to Crum's Preface. The Foreword is being reprinted in *Coptica*, journal of the Saint Mark Foundation and Saint Shenouda the Archimandrite Coptic Society, Los Angeles, 2006, forthcoming.

16. Stephen C. Carlson, *Hypotyposeis: Sketches in Biblical Studies*, http://www.hypotyposeis.org/weblog/2005/03/gospel-of-judas-in-news_29.html, "Gospel of Judas in the News, Last Updated: April 7, 2005."

17. James M. Robinson, "The Discovery of the Nag Hammadi Codices," *Biblical Archeologist* (42:4, Fall 1979): 206–24: 214.

18. Henk Schutten, "'Your life is at stake with this manuscript'" in the Dutch newspaper *Het Parool*, translated by Michel van Rijn on his Web site, http:www.michelvanrijn.nl/artnews/parool-trans1.htm (February 16, 2006), available also at http://www.tertullian.org/rpearse/manuscripts/gospel_of_judas/ (February 16, 2006).

19. The Dutch article, "Judasevangelie niet van Judas," listed "From Michel van Rijn, 1st April 2005, from http://www.katholieknieuwsblad.nl/," available also at http://www.tertullian.org/rpearse/manuscripts/gospel_of_judas/. The translation is no doubt by Van Rijn.

20. *The Facsimile Edition of the Nag Hammadi Codices: Introduction*, 21.

21. Michel van Rijn on his Web site, http:www.michelvanrijn.nl/artnews/, December 9, 2001, available at http://www.tertullian.org/rpearse/manuscripts/gospel_of_judas/ (February 16, 2006).

22. Hans-Gebhart Bethge, "The Letter of Peter to Philip," in *New Testament Apocrypha*, I: *Gospels and Related Writings* (ed. Wilhelm Schneemelcher; Louisville, Ky.: Westminster/John Knox, 1991), 342, and 347, n. 2.

23. Marvin W. Meyer, "NHC VIII,2: The Letter of Peter to Philip: Introduction," in *Nag Hammadi Codex VIII* (ed. John H. Sieber; The Coptic Gnostic Library; Nag Hammadi Studies 31; Leiden, New York, Copenhagen, Cologne: E. J. Brill, 1991), 227–32: 232. This statement is also to be found at the conclusion of the Introduction to *The Letter of Peter to Philip* in *The Nag Hammadi Library in English*.

24. Michel van Rijn on his Web site, http:www.michelvanrijn.nl/artnews/, September, 2001, available at http://www.tertullian.org/rpearse/manuscripts/gospel_of_judas/ (February 16, 2006).

25. Roger Thiede, "Das JUDAS-Evangelium," *FOCUS* 13 (March 26, 2005): 108–16.

26. Thiede, "Das JUDAS-Evangelium," 109.

27. Thiede, "Das JUDAS-Evangelium," 109.

28. Thiede, "Das JUDAS-Evangelium," 109–10.

29. Michel Van Rijn on his Web site, http:www.michelvanrijn.nl/artnews/ (February 16, 2006), available also at http://www.tertullian.org/rpearse/manuscripts/gospel_of_judas/ (February 16, 2006).

CHAPTER FIVE: THE PEDDLING OF *THE GOSPEL OF JUDAS*

1. Roger Thiede, "Das JUDAS-Evangelium," *FOCUS* 13, 2005, 110.

2. Ralph Pöhner, "Judas, der Held," *FACTS*, January 6, 2005, 78.

3. Robert Macalister Hall, "The Gospel Truth," in *The Independent on Sunday*, June 5, 2005, 26.

4. Pöhner, "Judas, der Held," 78.

5. Roberty, in his interview with Stacy Meichtry, Vatican correspondent of Religion News Service, February 13–14, 2006.

6. Michel Van Rijn, December 2004, on his Web site, http:www.michelvanrijn.nl/artnews/ (February 16, 2006), available also at http://www.tertullian.org/rpearse/manuscripts/gospel_of_judas/ (February 16, 2006).

7. Thiede, "Das JUDAS-Evangelium," 111.

8. Pöhner, "Judas, der Held," 78.

9. Michel van Rijn on his Web site, http:www.michelvanrijn.nl/artnews/ (February 16, 2006), available also at http://www.tertullian.org/rpearse/manuscripts/gospel_of_judas/ (February 16, 2006).

10. Michel van Rijn on his Web site, http:www.michelvanrijn.nl/artnews/ (February 16, 2006), available also at http://www.tertullian.org/rpearse/manuscripts/gospel_of_judas/ (February 16, 2006),

11. Apparently this letter, available on van Rijn's Web site, is the source of Pöhner's report, "Judas, der Held," 78:

> A few years later another American got involved in the matter: James Robinson. . . . With the Egyptian he agreed on a total price in the area of $900,000 and agreed on a meeting in New York.
>
> I never met the Egyptian, and did not agree on a price with him or Perdios.

12. In e-mails from Charles W. Hedrick to me dated January 24 and February 3, 2006.

13. Pöhner, "Judas, der Held," 77.

14. Charles W. Hedrick, "The ~~Four~~ 34 Gospels: Diversity and Division Among the Earliest Christians," *Bible Review* 18.3 (June 2002): 20–31, 46–47: 26; Charles W. Hedrick, "The Secret Gospel of Mark: Stalemate in the Academy," *Journal of Early Christian Studies* 11.2 (Summer 2003): 133–145: 139.

15. Pöhner, "Judas, der Held," 78–79.

16. Thiede, "Das JUDAS-Evangelium," 110.

17. Charles W. Hedrick and Paul Mirecki, *The Gospel of the Redeemer* (Santa Rosa, Calif.: Polebridge, 1999).

18. Available on the Web site of Michel van Rijn, April 27, 2005, http: www.michelvanrijn.nl/artnews/ (February 16, 2006), available also at http:// www.tertullian.org/rpearse/manuscripts/gospel_of_judas/ (February 16, 2006).

19. On his Web site www.MichelvanRijn.NL@artnews.

20. Thiede, "Das JUDAS-Evangelium," 111.

21. See the Web site of Michel van Rijn, April 8, 2005, http:www.michelvan-rijn.nl/artnews/ (February 16, 2006), available also at http://www.tertullian. org/rpearse/manuscripts/gospel_of_judas/ (February 16, 2006).

22. See the Web site of Michel van Rijn, December 9, 2001, http:www. michelvanrijn.nl/artnews/ (February 16, 2006), available also at http://www. tertullian.org/rpearse/manuscripts/gospel_of_judas/ (February 16, 2006).

23. Hall, "The Gospel Truth," 26.

24. Henk Schutten, "The hunt for the Gospel of Judas," Michel van Rijn on his Web site, http:www.michelvanrijn.nl/artnews/parool-trans1.htm (February 16, 2006), available also at http://www.tertullian.org/rpearse/manuscripts/ gospel_of_judas/ (February 16, 2006).

25. Thiede, "Das JUDAS-Evangelium," 111, 113.

26. Michel Van Rijn, on his Web site, December 2004, http:www. michelvanrijn.nl/artnews/ (February 16, 2006), available also at http://www. tertullian.org/rpearse/manuscripts/gospel_of_judas/ (February 16, 2006).

27. Thiede, "Das JUDAS-Evangelium," 113.

28. Thiede, "Das JUDAS-Evangelium," 113.

29. Thiede, "Das JUDAS-Evangelium," 114.

30. Thiede, "Das JUDAS-Evangelium," 114.

31. Schutten, "The hunt for the Gospel of Judas."

32. Schutten, "The hunt for the Gospel of Judas."

33. Hedrick, in an e-mail to me dated January 28, 2006.

34. Hedrick, in an e-mailed letter dated February 6, 2006.

35. Hedrick, in the e-mailed letter dated February 6, 2006.

36. Hedrick, in an e-mailed letter dated February 1, 2006.

37. Hedrick, in e-mailed letters dated February 6 and 18, 2006.

38. Hedrick, in an e-mail dated February 7, 2006.

39. Hedrick, in the e-mailed letter dated February 18, 2006.

40. Pöhner, "Judas, der Held," 77.

41. Thiede, "Das JUDAS-Evangelium, 112.

42. Thiede, "Das JUDAS-Evangelium, 113.

43. Schutten, "Is there a copy in the Vatican?" Michel Van Rijn, on his Web site, December 2004, http:www.michelvanrijn.nl/artnews/parool-trans1. htm (February 16, 2006), available also at http://www.tertullian.org/rpearse/ manuscripts/gospel_of_judas/ (February 16, 2006).

44. Schutten, "The shady side of the art trade."

45. Schutten, "The shady side of the art trade."

46. Roberty, in an interview with Stacy Meichtry, Vatican correspondent of Religion News Service, February 13–14, 2006.

47. Thiede, "Das JUDAS-Evangelium," 109: "16 x 29 cm."

48. Thiede, "Das JUDAS-Evangelium," 109.

CHAPTER SIX: THE PUBLICATION AND SIGNIFICANCE OF
THE GOSPEL OF JUDAS

1. Roberty, in the memorandum to Kaufman of December 15, 2000.

2. See my essay, "The Discovering and Marketing of Coptic Manuscripts: The Nag Hammadi Codices and the Bodmer Papyri," in *Sundries in honour of Torgny Säve-Söderbergh, Acta Universitatis Uppsaliensis, Boreas: Uppsala Studies in Ancient Mediterranean and Near Eastern Civilizations* 13 (1984): 97–114, reprinted in *The Roots of Egyptian Christianity*, eds. Birger A. Pearson and James E. Goehring, *Studies in Antiquity and Christianity* (Philadelphia: Fortress, 1986), 1–25; and *The Pachomian Monastic Library at the Chester Beatty Library and the Bibliothèque Bodmer*, Occasional Papers 19 (Claremont, Calif.: The Institute for Antiquity and Christianity, 1990), reprinted in *The Role of the Book in the Civilizations of the Near East, Manuscripts of the Middle East* 5 (1990–1991 [1993]): 26–40.

3. Michel Van Rijn's Web site, http://www.michelvanrijn.nl/artnews/ (February 16, 2006), available also at http://www.tertullian.org/rpearse/manuscripts/gospel_of_judas/ (February 16, 2006).

4. Michel Van Rijn, http://www.michelvanrijn.nl/artnews/ (February 16, 2006), available also at http://www.tertullian.org/rpearse/manuscripts/gospel_of_judas/ (February 16, 2006).

5. From the Web site of Michel van Rijn, April 27, 2005.

6. A preliminary draft entitled "From The Nag Hammadi Codices to *The Gospels of Mary and Judas*" was published in the Coptic newspaper *Watani International*, July 10, 2005, p. 2, ed. Saad Michael Saad. This was updated and presented in the panel on the theme "How Nag Hammadi Changed the World of Early Christianity," in the Nag Hammadi and Gnosticism Section of the Annual Meeting of the Society of Biblical Literature in Philadelphia on November 20, 2005. A minor updating of that paper was published in February, 2006, "From the Nag Hammadi Codices to *The Gospel of Mary* and *The Gospel of Judas*," Occasional Papers 48 (and Claremont, Calif.: The Institute for Antiquity and Christianity, 2006).

7. Patrick Jean-Baptiste, in *Sciences et Avenir*, 707 (January 2006): 38–45: "L'évangile de Judas," 38–40, and "Les tribulations d'un manuscrit apocryphe," 41–45.

8. Jean-Baptiste, "Les tribulations d'un manuscrit apocryphe," 41.

9. Jean-Baptiste, "L'évangile de Judas," 38.

10. From the interview by Roger Thiede with Stephen Emmel, entitled "Ein anderes Frühchristentum?" In *FOCUS* 13/2005 118–19: 119.

11. Ralph Pöhner, "Judas, der Held," *FACTS*, January 6, 2005, 79.

12. Pöhner, "Judas, der Held, 79.

13. Roger Thiede, "Das JUDAS-Evangelium," *FOCUS* 13, 2005, 114–15.

14. Stephen C. Carlson, "Gospel of Judas in the News, Last Updated: April 7, 2005." http://www.hypotyposeis.org/weblog/2005/03/gospel-of-judas-in-news_29.html

15. Pöhner, "Judas, der Held," 79.

16. Summarized in James M. Robinson, *The Gospel of Jesus* (San Francisco: HarperSanFrancisco, 2005), 75–77.

17. Robert H. Eisenman and James M. Robinson, eds., *A Facsimile Edition of the Dead Sea Scrolls* (Washington, D.C.: Biblical Archaeology Society, 1991, second revised impression 1992).

18. For full details see James M. Robinson, *The French Rôle in Early Nag Hammadi Studies 1946–1953*, Bibliothèque copte de Nag Hammadi, section Études (Leuven: Peeters, forthcoming), and, abbreviated, "The French Role in Early Nag Hammadi Studies," *The Journal of Coptic Studies* 7 (2005): 1–12.

19. *La Bourse Égyptienne*, June 10, 1949.

20. *The Nag Hammadi Library in English*, eds. James M. Robinson and Marvin W. Meyer (Leiden: E. J. Brill, 1977, and San Francisco: Harper & Row, 1977).